Chocolate Flavored

Chocolate Flavored

A collection of Poems and Short Stories

Karlene Robinson

iUniverse, Inc.

New York Lincoln Shanghai

Chocolate Flavored
A collection of Poems and Short Stories

iUniverse books may be ordered through booksellers or by contacting:

iUniverse
2021 Pine Lake Road, Suite 100
Lincoln, NE 68512
www.iuniverse.com
1-800-Authors (1-800-288-4677)

ISBN-13: 978-0-595-39220-9 (pbk)
ISBN-13: 978-0-595-67676-7 (cloth)
ISBN-13: 978-0-595-83611-6 (ebk)
ISBN-10: 0-595-39220-2 (pbk)
ISBN-10: 0-595-67676-6 (cloth)
ISBN-10: 0-595-83611-9 (ebk)

Printed in the United States of America

Dedicated to my children
Taisha and Jevon
For inspiring me to live life everyday

In loving memory of my grandfather
Nathaniel McLeod
Who instilled within me dignity, morals and principles

Contents

He said…

A Man's Heart

Last night he said…

The moans I made the other night
They were coming from deep within my heart
The way I moved it's because of you
No other girl has me this way
The way I held you
My heart melted
MY GOD
I don't deserve you
You're heaven sent
Are you feeling me too?
Are you sure?
Do you want me as your man?
Forever more?
The kisses I gave you
From your head to your toes
The way you screamed my name
I knew you wanted more
I kissed you like that Because it was you
No other girl gets that from this dude
Are you feeling me too?
You sure?
Do you want me as your man?
Forever more?
I love you baby
Do you hear me?
I love you girl
Stay with me

Stop Talking

Stop talking to your friends
I don't like them
Why they all up in our business?

That's why they don't have a man
That's why they never gonna have one
That's why they never liked the way I treated you
That's why they say the things they do

Stop talking to your friends
Telling them our business
Telling them our arguments
Telling them…
You keep telling them…
Everything!!

She said you should leave me
Didn't she?
She thinks I'm gonna play you
Like she got played
Don't she?

But see…

I'm different
And so are you
I'd rather be dead
If I tried to play you
You don't put up with bull
So tell your friends
Leave us alone

Baby stop talking to your friends
Stop telling them our business

Baby please
This relationship is just between
You and Me

The Down Low

Hi, it's me
Don't know where to start or How to begin
I don't know how to approach you lady

             His voice shook hard
              As he said the words:
Don't think I am weak
I'm just feeling ya'
Don't think I am not a man
I'm really just feeling ya'

See a brother like me
All macho to my friends
Tough with my crew
Fight a battle to the end
Yea girl
That's me, you know how I get down
But when I'm with you
I want the soft side of me to be shown

Think I don't think of the arguments we have
It bothers me
As it bothers you
Beneath me I too am human
Beneath my tattoo on my chest of this gun
Is a heart just for you
In diamonds and gold

Ah, let me stop
What's wrong with me

Geeze girl
You got me all hooked and sh…Shouldn't be like this though

My boys would laugh
Wouldn't they?
Your mouth is curved
You laughing too
Can't wait to tell your girls Ah?

That's alright
That's the point where I'm at
I don't care
Go ahead
It's all good

You know
What I'm really trying to say
Is…Ah
Baby, you see
I'm in love with you girl
Trust me
This nigga's real

Experience

Why can't you believe me?
He asked her desperately
Because he had wronged her a thousand times
Lied
Connived
Betrayed her trust for the pleasures of a night
Why can't you believe me?
The past is the past
And the past has passed
Let it remain in the days of old
Why?
Tell me!
Do you want me?
Marry me...
Will you?

How can you?
Not seeing that I have changed
I am not the man that played
Your heart like a guitar
Strumming
Strumming
Playing
A sad tune is what you know
Now I'll show you
My love is true

You ever seen a man like me?
You never seen true love so real
I'll take you high amidst the clouds
I'll let you bellow my name out loud

I'll trample on your zones within
The woman in you I will reveal
I'll take you far away from doubts
I'll show you what true love is about

Cause you see, I'm sorry
Believe me Just this once
Hold me
Let's forget the past is the past
And the past has passed

She said…

Ain't I Still A Woman

Though I don't have a man
I am still a Woman
And on Valentine's Day I don't get a card
I am a Woman
And at Easter I go alone to Church on Sunday
Yet I am a Woman
And at Christmas I roam the street all day
I am still a Woman

'Cause don't need a man
To tell me good night honey
Or Merry Christmas

I don't need a man
To give me a ring

I just need to love me first

A man is good
But if I ain't got one
Ain't I Still a Woman?

Chocolate Flavored

My self-esteem is not low
It is just hard to believe
I have finally found
The man of my dreams

A chocolate flavored brother
Like no other
He is one of a kind
But I know he's mine
My poem's kind a silly isn't it?
I know
but you're not the one who's feeling it
Feeling it
Feeling it

He tantalizes taste buds
To make you believe he'll melt
In your mouth not in your hands
He's without nuts and raisins
The brother is chocolate flavored

He kisses slow
But passionately
He takes all roads
towards your womanly delicacies
when he moves it's with rhythm
slowly, slowly
it's condemning to other men of course
The way he is
Just the way he is
The way he kiss

Just the way he kiss
The way he touches and caresses
He trapped me
With his innocence

Can it be real
Is this for real?
Silly of me asking these questions
Acting all childish
Blaming it on love
I've never met another man
To him there's no second
I'm in love I know it
I'm the one who's feeling it
Feeling it

Defeated

If I tell you that I love you
Will you believe?
If I tell you that there is a fire
Blazing within
Is there a source to quench?
After all
It's only been what?
Three months
Since I know you
They say true love takes time to grow
If that's true
My love grew
before you were born
Because I yearn
To be with you
Again
I yearn to feel you within
Again
Again
Once more I yearn
Oh quench the blaze
That my soul arrest
Are you feeling the same?
At nights do you fantasize
And call me by name?
Do you visualize?
Can you even sympathize-
With me—
Is this where you want to be?
Tell me

Whisper softly in my ear
The silence of my ear-
-drum

That's what my heart is beating like
That's what my soul wants to move to
The rhythm of the drum in the night
A drum starting softly
hand caressing the carcass
and moving steadily against its harshness
and pulsating with the beat and the rhythm
and the rhythm and the beat
with your touch—
Then I am defeated

Love?

I think I'm in love
No really I do
Do you think its possible
To love again, do you?
He's wonderful
I mean I know he must have faults
But the way I feel for him
I know this one will last
I really can't explain it well
But the feeling—is driving me crazy!
He says he loves me
I know he's for real
But so much doubt's within me—

Not because of him
But because of my past
I've been wronged so many times
I'm afraid to be wronged again
But he says he loves me
I know it's true
The way he looks at me
The way that he does

I really think I love him
I really do
Pray for me and him
That our love will last

And that this time
It's true-

—love?

You
Think?

I didn't think I could do it
After you walk out of my life
I didn't think I could see it
Someone else being your wife

I didn't think I could cope
After you took all my hope
From within me
I didn't think it was a possibility
I didn't think
I didn't fathom the unthinkable
To me that is
That we wouldn't be a couple
I didn't conceive the incredible
Thoughts of being separable

I didn't want to believe
That you and I was just a dream
Figment of our imagination
For better or worse
In any situation

Cause here we are strangers again
Here we are no emotions within
For each other we have no feelings

I didn't think this was possible
I didn't think

I did not think

NO MORE DRAMA—RAMA

Just a note to say good-bye,
To the many times you called me a B*W***.
To the times no matter how hard I tried
You were never satisfied.
I could have called the cops 'cause they'd be glad
To take a brother like you
Handcuff a fool like you
To the times you said I wasn't no good
Wouldn't be no good
The times my tears would stain my face
The time my pain became a familiar place
Many times my lips kissed your fist
Then my thirst quenched by my blood
Too many times I was left alone
No comfort, No home
So this letter says Good-bye to the DRAMA—RAMA
The Soap Opera
The Schizophrenia
The 'sorrys' the "baby I love you'
After being whipped by you
Don't mean Sugar Honey Ice Tea
Cause when you made love
I felt raped viciously
And you thought it all Good?
So read on my brother Find you another
B*W***

Queen of Africa

I'm the Queen of the Motherland

Africa Land
Soul Land
The beasts of the field obey my commands

The sun extends its rays
Upon me every dawn

The green grass beneath my feet
Withers not

The mountains roar as I pass them by

The rain blesses my head
With the dews from the sky

My enemies crumble at my very shadow
and fall at my feet

And though they see me not

My presence alone defeats

Yes I rise to Africa
To see the vastness of its land
I welcome the Motherland

I'm the Queen

Beautified Essence

From its Origin

Today

Today I just want to run away
and not look back

Not be a mother today
Not be a woman today
                    No

Today I just want to hide
Not appreciating bills today
That proves my independence
Today I just want to forget my name
I just want to become someone else

Who doesn't know pain
Doesn't know shame
Doesn't recognize the game
Of the players around

But I must go on
I wish life had a pause button
To stop and go and go and stop
And stop and stop

But life must go on
And I must conquer on
And I must be a mother
A woman
        A strong woman who is a mother

Believe in ME

I want to believe in you
I want to see the truth in your words
That echoes from your heart
That gives me joy as they impart

Your lips

Is what I behold
Each time I see your face
Each time you stand in my way

I want to believe in you
I yearn to see the truth in your words
That echoes from your heart
That gives me joy as they impart

Your lips

I long to believe
I long to achieve my desire
To believe in you

Because you believe in me
Don't you?

i

i remember the day *i* saw your face
Amidst the crowd in the restaurant

You sipped your soup
i watched your youth-
-ful lips sipping the soup

i wanted you then
and *i* want you now

i remember the time
The very first time you kissed my lips
i melted
i knew right then
You were heaven sent

i wanted you then
and *i* want you now

the time you took your hands
and explored me
the time you took your tongue
and caressed me
the time you took your inner man
and seduced me
you seduced me

i wanted you then
and *i* want you now

i remember quite well
You seduced me

wanted you then
and want you now

In the Night

I was afraid to let him know
That I feared the night
I feared the shadows that danced on the wall
Or maybe in my head

I held him close
So close I felt his breath in my lungs
He thought it was love
I knew it was fear
of the night appearing

I held his waist against me
and I felt his life within
The night crept upon us
My strength beside me lay still

And I felt his breath
I felt his life
I knew I was safe
At the break of night

He thought it was love
That made me laugh
I knew it was fear
of the creeping night

I wanted to tell him
But his ego prevailed
He thought it was love
His ego prevailed

But the night came
And went
And I knew tomorrow

Repeat
Repeat
Repeat

Voice-mail

I'm trying to call you
but you're not answering
it's things like this
That gets frustrating
Your cell phone
Your beeper
Your house phone
Your two-way pager
Are they on?
Come on—
—Tell me what's going on!

My mind is leading me negatively
My soul is telling me
That you're just busy
What should I believe?
See I've got certain pet peeves
I hate it
Can never understand it
When a man won't answer me

Explain it to me
What is going on
Am I too obsessive with you
What am I doing wrong?

Hello?
Yea I knew so
It's your voice-mail again
But that's alright though
This is my last call

I know I've said it before
But believe me
Yea believe me
I really ain't calling no mo'

Hello?
Hello?

I-N

Sometimes I just think of how it will be
To kiss you
But I know a lady ain't suppose to think like that
Sometimes I think of how it will be
When you come closer to me
But I know a lady ain't suppose to think like that

I want to know how it will be
To feel your manliness within me
To become you
and you become me
When the clouds above welcome us
And we are blessed
With the explosion of curiosity

They say it killed the cat
Kill me then
I maybe will like that
You think?
Maybe
I feel you against me
Are you welcoming me?

Passion-
—That's what I need
Without you caring how I feel-
—But in a good way
So don't pardon my screams
Just passion me
Make me into a woman that's real
That will believe

That your manhood was worth my time
My hour, my minute
With you in it
In it
In my minute

Yes worth my seconds
With you in it
In it

Dominique Jean

I truly had given up
Dominique Jean
I truly had thought
making passionate love
Was just a movie scene

Seen it
Never did it
'Cause it never happened to me

Me
Being the one
Always a victim
To love
Unreal

Unreal thoughts coming through
Wanted a real man like you
Searched but just gave up
Then you appeared
Luck?

Luckily you're available
Dominique Jean
What should we do?
Doing this thing like a child
'Cause you got me all wrapped up
Screaming
Moaning
Going wild
While you're just cool
Watching me

Feeling me
Teasing me
With your sincerity
Building my inner curiosity
To levels I thought impossible,
Dominique Jean

Jean...

It was one of those things
A never planned thing
When things just happened

Co Workers
Becoming coworkers
If you know what I mean

He was a smooth talker
Grab my heart like a stalker
Didn't want to let go
Or maybe I didn't want to let go
Who knows?

Like Mary J. Blige
I couldn't believe
This love thing
A never planned thing
Just happened
I lost me
He
Really didn't say much
It was really a touch
On my hand

It was one of those things
A never planned thing

Reality Check…

Child Support

She said:
"Did I hear you correctly?
The child ain't yours?"

"Oh yeah niggah we'll see
Child support gonna be plenty
Yeah
You heard me"

He said: "Oh it's like that?"

"Yeah niggah
The white man gonna rumble in your paycheck

Didn't have to be like this
—You took it there
Don't even try to play yo'self
This chick ain't going on no welfare

Whatever niggah
'Cause see, now I ain't feeling ya
Talk to the Judge at the Family Court
That's where I'll be seeing ya

Twenty dollars?
That ain't good enough
Pamper cost more than that

Niggah don't play yo'self
This chick ain't on crack

When you met me I was fly
You ain't gonna see nothing less

Whatever drugs you're on
Better get Rehab help

Didn't use a condom
'Cause niggah I trusted you
But tomorrow I gotta check myself
Gave me a baby may gimme AIDS too
Ain't blaming ya
See I'm to blame
Don't sleep with dogs
They can't bark your name
My baby will live
With or without you
I'll be a mother and
Father too

I'll hold my own
But you gonna pay yours though
See ya soon niggah
At the Family Court"

Okay, Let's Talk

I do apologize for the immaturity yesterday
I am just afraid of getting hurt
I really do care for you
I love you very much
I can't deal with this feeling right now
You are breaking me down too much

I am scared as hell
I have never felt this way before
and I am very, very afraid
So what am I really trying to say is:

I can't fight this feeling anymore
I give in okay
I am yours to do whatever you want
I am in total control of your command okay
Because I totally give up

You have me thinking about you like crazy
You have my heart so weak—very weak
So I cannot fight
I don't have the strength to fight anymore okay

So here I am okay.

Just Another Brother

He was just walking like everyone else
wasn't even talking to himself
Yet,
they came rolling like he robbed a bank
told him to spread his legs
and jabbed him in his back
They
searched for something
anything to keep him
They
wanted to arrest him
to create a record for him
They
wanted to tarnish another brother's record
They
wanted to add him to society's number
They
called him a liar while checking his identity
They
told him he was the niggah
who committed petty larceny
They
tried to convince him he was guilty
and then told him
They
could make it easy if he confessed quickly
he thought he was dreaming
he'd seen it before
read it before
heard it before

now he had it knocking at his door
it wasn't a stranger's story anymore
he was living it
couldn't believe it
then the nightmare it ended
but he wanted to defend it
but he knew he was only a brother on a street
he knew he had to take it
he knew they had fake it
just because he was another brother on the street

FrIends

We're just friends-
Though I hate to see you go

We're just friends-
Yet inside I love you so

We're just friends
And that's all I ever want
It's more important for me to know

We're just friends
Though the love we made
The stars can't outshine the glow

The moon will never outdo the shapes
Our love takes
When we explode
Between the sheets
And we each meet our needs

And we fall amidst cloud nine
And I wish you were mine

But then I know

We're just friends
Though inside I want more

We're just friends
Though inside I want more
We're just friends
And that's all I ever want
It's more important to me

To be
Your friend

Just Friends

Kings Street

The first time I saw a white man
I was six or seven years old
That was back in my country
Walking on downtown Kingston Jamaica's asphalt road
Their mild mannerism amazed me
And the gentleness of their kind
The warmth among the many
That strolled and giving freely to me their smiles

But that was in my country
When they left their homeland cold
Their frigid temperatures
And ice frozen streets
To steal our sunshine gold
For when I came to visit
Their land of opportunity
The many white folks tripled
But no smiles were given freely
My big sister, Jackie,
Whispered in my ear
"The smiles we saw back then
they practiced them long before they came"
the ones who did smile
gave us half-a-one
and then walked briskly away
But as we looked behind us
Their smile had gone
Very quickly it had disappeared
My big sister turned her brows way up high
And opened wide her eyes

And with a nod I knew she said
"Thought that I had lied?"
"Did the white man not like us?"
I ask my sister, for she knew
"Yes, he did in our country, because he knows
He'll leave in a week or two
But when we come to his land
They do not like us then
Because they know we came to stay
And we'll grow old with them."

SHINE BLACK WOMAN

NOTHING CAN MAKE YOU BEAUTIFUL
NOTHING CAN MAKE YOU SHINE
ONLY YOU THAT IS EXCEPTIONAL
CAN ALLOW YOURSELF TO GLOW BRIGHT

LOOK IN THE MIRROR
SEE WHO YOU SEE
IT'S YOU BLACK WOMAN
AFRICA'S GEM GLOWING RADIANTLY

LOVE YOURSELF
BE PROUD TO BE
DIFFERENT THAN ANYONE ELSE
YOU'RE YOU, NOT HER, NOT ME

NOW RISE BLACK WOMAN
RISE TO GREET THE SUN
SING LOUD BLACK WOMAN
LET THE WHOLE WORLD KNOW
YOUR BEAUTY'S GLOWING NOW

Sista

A true '*Sista*' is—
A progressive '*Sista*' is—
One who displays the quality
Of surviving negativity

A '*Sista*' is one who can stand alone
Never leaning on anyone
One who knows just who she is
Loving each one of her differences

Who wins victoriously
Despite the odds
Never afraid of admitting her wrongs
Who gives to her child unselfishly
Working hard to be all she could be

A '*Sista*' is colorless
No particular skin tone
You're a true '*Sista*'
Stand tall and proud

Smelling the Coffee yet?

Guess you never thought I would
Never thought I could
Get up
And Leave

Guess you never thought I'd be strong
Never thought I could rise again

Guess you never think
For a minute
I could see my life
Without you in it

Guess you still can't believe
Guess you thought it a dream?

Wake up
Smelling the Coffee yet?

Out of the Pen

How do I deal with a brother
Who has just let loose from the pen
When his emotions run wild
Sometimes
I just sit down and cry
And wonder why
Did I get stuck with a brother
That just got loose from the pen

How do I give him security
To know I will always be here?
How do I comfort the pain that stabs him at night
I just want to hold him and let him cry
But I cry instead

Because he has been hardened by the system
Proven guilty before conviction
Left to die behind bars of steal
A raw deal
But it was real

God!
How?
How do I deal with a brother who has just been let loose
From the pen?
He has to learn again
To trust again
To learn again
To be a man again
But the system didn't teach him
The system lied to him

Saying you'll be fine again
Just go out and live again
They lied to him
Because he has to learn again
To love again

My brother man
How do I deal?

Short Stories...

A Flower is a Flower is a Flower

Dear Taisha,

Life for me began on June 14th, 1987 in a small room at Kings County Hospital. Two nurses and MommyRee witnessed the joy that would stay with me until this day. My happiness was a 'bundle of joy' that weighed seven pounds and fourteen ounces. My gladness had wrinkles all over it. It measured nineteen inches. The treasure I held in my hand, I named Taisha. Thank you for giving me a reason to live.

We never spoke of my childhood in depth before. That is because I waited for the right time to do it. Well I am taking the time to tell you of the role you played in my life and how grateful I am for you. God gave me a gift that no one else could give. He blessed me with you not only as a daughter, but also as a friend. I know you are a gift because of the relationship we have though you are only thirteen years old.

At fifteen years old I migrated from Jamaica. Auntie Jackie did not come with me to the United States of America. I felt lonely and abandoned. Auntie Jackie was my only true friend. I confided in her and told her my deepest secrets. I knew I could trust her.

Jackie was two years older than me. She was my mentor. When I left Jamaica a part of me remained with your aunt. Nothing could fill the emptiness I felt inside. Though we spoke a lot on the phone and we wrote to each other often, yet I was sad within. When you were born everything changed. With you in my life I experienced the same feeling I felt as a child in my sister's presence.

I became pregnant two years after coming to America. MommyRee had a small oak coffee table in the center of our living room. We lived on Washington Avenue in Brooklyn. Our apartment was small. The living room and kitchen shared space, which was also my bedroom. At nights I knelt on the coffee table and prayed, because the sofa bed occupied three quarter of the space in the room. I could have prayed on the bed but the springs felt uncomfortable against my knee, so the table became my altar.

I hoped for a girl. I yearned for a friend. I asked the Lord for a little girl who would love me unconditionally. Two months later I found out that half of my prayer was answered. The sonogram revealed my baby was a girl. The sonogram is a television that views the inside a woman's stomach when she is pregnant.

Thirteen years later, I found out that all of my prayer was answered.

You took your first step at ten months old. You held on to the round coffee table in our living room and danced to the music of Sesame Street. I left the room briefly to finish cooking. Upon reentering the room I noticed that you no longer stood by the table. You were about a foot away. You took your first step searching for me. When you saw me your mouth curved into a smile. Your eyes beamed with joy. Your arms were outstretched as you tried to quicken your pace. You were anxious to come closer to me. A deep feeling of need filled my soul. I lifted you up to my shoulder and your tiny fingers gripped my shirt.

Two weeks later you said your first word. The sauce, made of pear, remained on the outer parts of your lips. You held your fingers high above your head to observe them. You started banging on the tray of your highchair. As I moved closer to wipe the excess fruit that decorated the white tray with yellow spots you said "ma, ma". And with rhythm you said it faster. No other word sounded sweeter to me.

The Lord answered my cry that cold day in November as I knelt before him in prayer. I proved it many times. When you were five years old you had a desire to go to church. I sent you to church with our neighbor, Donna. Several Sundays later you came home from Church sad. You told me all your friends' mommies went to church with them except your mommy. You convinced me to go with you. Two Sundays later I gave my life to the Lord.

I found peace, joy and happiness in God. Many times you tell me what a great mom I am. But without God it would not be possible to be a great mom. Each day when I lift my hands to thank Jesus for saving me, I thank him for you. Every Sunday as I worship, I give thanks to the Lord for allowing you to be used by him to beckon me to his presence.

Sometimes I feel like quitting. Or other times I feel like taking a 'vacation' from church. But you inspire me to 'fight the good fight of faith'. You remind me that the world has nothing to offer. You encourage me to continue reaching for my goals and tell me everything will be okay. With you as a daughter Taisha, I am always proud to be a mother.

You were nine years old when I had Jevon. Words cannot express my grati- tude for the help you offered. I became ill from morning sickness. You gave me water constantly and removed cups and plates from my bedroom. You emptied the garbage, or you sat beside me to rub my stomach. When I was too dizzy to use the remote to turn on the television you did the task with a smile. Those are things that I treasure.

When he was born you assisted me in every way. You were eager to learn how to change his diapers. You were anxious to feed him. You helped me in purchasing his clothes. You became his angel on earth too. How can we ever say thank you Taisha? Too few letters make up both words.

Since then you have helped me to care for your brother. At times I was too lenient in disciplining him. As though you were the mother you replied, "Mommy you shouldn't do that", or "Mommy you shouldn't let him do that". I value your opinion. You are very mature with your decisions. You are very honest with your words.

The Bible tells of tithing. I did not have a conviction for it. You did not have a job, yet each Sunday you tithed ten percent of your allowance. The Bible says in the last days children shall lead. You taught me how to be obedient to the word of God. You showed me that faith produces blessings.

Two Christmas' ago you had a list of things you wanted. I was not working enough money to get you everything you desired. Though no one knew about, you received everything you wrote on the paper. At eleven years old this is what you said, "See Mommy if you tithe too, you will receive as much as I did".

I have found a friend in you Taisha. You cleaned the house without being asked. You washed the dishes spontaneously. That means a lot to me especially when I am tired after work.

I remember the day when I left work early without you knowing. I wanted to surprise you. But instead I was surprise.

There you were in the living room with a broom in your hand. You were slouched over picking up bits of paper off the floor. You were startled as I entered the house. But I was surprised to see you cleaning. You were not expecting me home until two hours later. Nevertheless, you were considerate enough to help with the chores of our home though you were not asked.

I am the proudest mom at the Parents' Teachers' Conferences. They always remarked on your progress in your academic work. But the thing that made me glow with pride was their comments on your attitude in school. They commended you highly for your mannerism. I am glad to know not only in my presence are you well spoken, but also in my absence.

I appreciate the support you have given me this semester. My first year in college and it was hectic. But you kept telling me "Mom you can do it". When I felt as though my strength was gone you cheered me on to the finish line. You always knew what to say and when to say it. You are my best friend.

Remember when I wanted to change jobs? I hesitated for two weeks. I asked a lot of 'what ifs'. You told me to pray about it. You told me to have faith. You said it was a blessing from God because he wanted me to go to church on Sundays. I never got the weekend off from my previous job. Now I am glad I took your advice. My new job pays for my tuition at school and gives me more vacation time. But best of all, their health benefit package is superb.

You encouraged me to get a car. I wanted to get a used car. You insisted for us to get a new one. I am glad I took your suggestion. Everything you craved for, I watched as the Lord blessed you with it. Your faith has taught me the value of believing in things that seems unachievable.

Aunt Jackie became temporarily paralyzed in August. Your first cousin Kimberly was depressed. You decided to go to Jamaica for the entire summer to keep her company while her mother was in the hospital. That was a nice thing you did. I am sure it helped Kim to deal with the situation better. Auntie Jackie said you helped her a whole lot too. She said you gave her everything she wanted but could not get because she could not walk. I never expressed my sincere thanks to you about this before, so here I am expressing it now.

When I look in our albums I marvel at how you have grown. I never felt lonely after you were born. I never needed any one else as a friend because you became my buddy. When you smile, even when I am sad, you cheer me up instantly.

The little girl that saw no wrong in me now truthfully tells me my faults. I praise your sincerity. What I applaud most is the respect that it is done with. You never forget the fact that I am your mother. And even though we confide in each other about many things we still do not disrespect our mother-daughter relationship. Remember the time I asked you to tell the person on the phone that I was not home. Yes, I actually asked you to lie for me. You replied, "Mommy then don't answer the phone. Or just tell them you don't want to talk". I never asked you to loose your integrity again. And you taught me to reevaluate mine.

It was my birthday. You must have saved up your allowance for months to be able to buy my gift. When I came home the house was immaculate. In the center of the table in the dining room was a medium sized gift bag. A card stuck out of the bag. You came in the kitchen and wished me a happy birthday.

I was impressed by the gifts you chose. Among the gifts were a pen and a small notebook. You said you knew I enjoyed writing. But the best gift was the postcard you gave me. The words were beautiful. Your personal inscription lay upon my heart for days. You wrote, "Mommy I may not always say I love you often enough but I do".

Growing up in Jamaica things are different than in America. Birthdays were usually celebrated once every five years, if at all. Four years ago you went to a

Hallmark store with your Aunt Janice. You bought me a card a month before my birthday. I thought you forgot my date of birth. But you replied that Janice wanted to buy you something and you chose to buy the card instead. You did not know if you would have money when my birthday came, so you bought it then. The card had my name on it. It meant so much to me.

There are many people that I have known at different times in my life that made a difference. My Sunday school teacher taught me that God died for me on Calvary. Grandpa told me he loved me each night before I went to sleep. Auntie Jackie was my best friend. My English professor at Nassau College spoke with wisdom when he said you should seek someone who you can love instead of someone who will love you.

I never understood what he meant until I wrote it. When you seek someone to love, you look for someone of character. You will choose someone who has the same morals, values and beliefs as you. But when you look for someone to love you, usually you seek out of desperation. When I prayed to God for a little girl, I wanted someone to love. When you entered my life thirteen years ago you gave me all of these. You showed me what God can do. Before we go to sleep each night you tell me you love me. You are the best friend a mother could ask for in a daughter.

Each day as I watch you grow, you are like a flower. As it opens the real beauty of its petals are seen. Each petal is a representation of your characteristics. The color brightens as the flower matures. Your color is your character. I will nurture you with my love as the flower is nurtured with water.

I wish I could protect you from the cold and cruel world out there. But every time we speak I am convinced that you will be strong enough. I want to give you everything you desire. Each time you discuss your views of life, I am persuaded that you will be ambitious enough to be the best you can be. You have given me new meanings to love, life and happiness.

Love, Mom

A Child's Thought
An essay by T. Shay

For as long as I have known myself I had a Barbie doll and a Ken doll. They were married and had the perfect American life—a mansion, a car, careers, vacations and money. But most of all they had love. They were married for 43 years, but now their separation made news. Barbie and Ken were getting divorced.

It seems as if other elements are key factors of marriages in the decade in which we live and love no longer plays an important role. The US Census Bureau reported that 'nearly half of recent first marriages may end in divorce' and that 'first marriages which end in divorce last 7 to 8 years on an average'. Www.divorcereform.org states that Massachusetts has the lowest divorce rate and Nevada has the highest. After having first hand experience of a divorce in progress between my mother and her now ex-husband and seeing the statistics I agree that marriages should be entered into as a contract that is renewable in increments of 5 years.

The toughest years of a marriage are the first 5 years. These years are the 'getting to know you' years. When one realizes that the beauty or prince that they married indeed have faults. After the honeymoon has ended, toilet seat remains up and hair is left on the bathroom sink, or the fact that during their courtship ideas and opinions were put aside to accommodate a kiss or a hug. But now living together differences are more apparent. Regardless that love is playing a part in the hearts of these two people, they are still in fact strangers learning to familiarize themselves with each other. Learning to tolerate and accept the fact that the cover of the toothpaste maybe left off sometimes but it is too trivial to argue about. Or learning that make up was worn whenever they went out on a date, but it cannot be worn to bed. Therefore appearance in the morning will differ from the Saturday night date.

Marriages should be renewable after a five-year period. If individuals decide to separate in between periods then divorce would then be an option.

The Result

Norris asked me to accompany him to get the result of his AIDS test. Anxiously he paced the floor of the small clinic located in an isolated area of Kings County Hospital. Finally the nurse called him into her office. As he emerged he handed me a piece of paper with the outcome. Then he freight trained from the building. Hesitantly I examined the rectangular shaped white document with perforated edges. Norris tested positive for AIDS.

Three months after he found out that he carried the virus Norris disappeared from my life. For many months I questioned his friends of his whereabouts, but without success. Norris seemed worried the last time I saw him, though he denied it. Since then I learned to accept the truth about his medical condition.

A year later I received a call from Kings County Hospital AIDS center. Norris had given them my phone number in the case of an emergency two months prior when he was admitted. I had an appointment with them in the morning because his condition had worsened. I feared going to see him because I did not know what to expect.

As I followed the directions I received the day before it lead me to a narrow passageway. Tiles no longer decorated the floor. Instead concrete held the weight beneath my body. The dry cracks on the wall showed evidence that a coat of paint was needed. Cobwebs dangled from the corners of the walls. This section of the hospital seemed deserted. The stillness of everything scared me.

Huge numbers identified the rooms on their entrances. The door with number 307 was ajar. The person lying on the bed was still. A white sheet was draped tightly around their feet. I braced my body forward halfway through the door as I peeked to see if the patient was Norris. Tubes seemed to exit every hole on the person's body. I was startled as the nurse entered the room. She adjusted the IV on his arm. "He often spoke of suicide when he could speak", the nurse whispered softly as if she dreaded him hearing her. Then she left the room.

The bones of his face were more prominent. His body seemed to disappear between the sheets. He had lost a vast amount of weight. His lips were swollen. His face had many sores, some of which were healed. The smell of the room caused me to feel dizzy. As I looked around the room for a chair my eyes glanced his charts. To everyone in the hospital he was 'Chart # 343421'.

The nurse returned with her supervisor. She explained that within a week his health had deteriorated rapidly. She disclosed that Norris was gay and he requested that no one be contacted until his death was sure. I was hurt but I hid my pain. I signed all the appropriate papers. They left me alone again.

I stared blankly at him on his bed as I ruminated. Five years ago on this same date, Norris and I went to lunch. His giggles illuminated any dark room. Now he lay awaiting death. Though I was scared, I moved slowly and kissed his forehead, something I never thought possible—kissing someone with the virus.

In the past we discussed the consequences of AIDS. I urged him eight years ago to get tested for the virus when I took my first test. He laughed and said that AIDS was a homosexual disease. He lied that he loved women, and never dated a man before. Now here he was with the 'homosexual' disease, or so everyone thinks. How many lives will it claim before everyone realize that it is not partial to age, sex, ethnicity, or financial status?

Looking at Norris one more time before exiting the room I decided to get tested again. Leaving the trail of hallway behind me, tears trickled down my cheeks. I never wanted to return to this section of Kings County Hospital Center again. Its bleakness reminded me of the disease itself and the segregation you face when you are tested positive with the AIDS virus.

People with the virus are often times scorned and feared because of the 'risks' of contracting the disease if they are touched. Ironically, unprotected sex and use of drugs with contaminated needles are approached with less caution than getting close to a person known to have HIV. Norris chose to die in the absence of his family. It haunted me for several months.

The vivid memory of Norris' withered body led me back to the small clinic to get tested again. As the needle pierced my skin, and the blood was drawn, I silently prayed and hoped to be negative.

Two days later I went for my result.

My heart fluttered from fear.

As I walked in the nurse's office a huge bulge formed in my throat. She asked should I test positive, was there someone to care for my children? Reality suddenly sank in of all the unprotected sex I had ever exposed myself to. Then she handed me the paper with my result.

Her voice magnified as she confirmed I tested negative.

From Gutter to Glory
An excerpt from "From Gutter to Glory"
[Unpublished]
A novel by Karlene Robinson

Being a single mom was not as I thought it would be. I had custody of my two children, Alethia and Jevon. Alethia was the oldest. My day repeated itself each morning—took Jevon to the babysitter, took Alethia to school and then went to work. In the evening it was just the reverse. I didn't have a life. Not that I didn't want one but I couldn't—not with two children. My mom lived on the level above me. She helped as much as she could, but I hated intruding on her time.

The only other help I received came from Steven. He had been my friend for years. He was my best friend. Doug hated the fact that I spoke to Steven as often as I did. I had stopped communicating with Steven as frequently as I use to because that's what Doug had wanted. But I always did yearn to be with Steven though he was a player—he had a girl for each day of the week. He was a successful black man who worked for a very prestigious company. He assisted me as much as he could. But with his BUSY, very Bih-ZEE schedule, well? You guess. He helped whenever he could.

"Let's go Jevon, please hurry, mommy gonna be late for work", I was never early for work. No matter how early I got up I was always late. Furthermore, I went to bed extremely late. I spent the entire night chatting online. Being new online was an adventure that I found greatly exhilarating. I had gone to the computer store in the community to get a free trial disk.

I could not believe it was already the break of dawn. I did not want to get up but I knew I had to. It was difficult getting out of bed and I wished I could remain sleeping, but reality came with my daughter repeatedly telling me to get up. She hated going school late especially on Mondays.

As I finished getting Jevon dressed, I remembered that I had left the car parked across the street because I was unable to park in front of the apartment before 7:00 p.m. I had decided not to wait until 7:00 p.m. after I returned from the computer store. Now I would have to cross the busy street to get to the car. I lived on a Boulevard that led to a highway, the Grand Central Parkway.

"Let's go people", I shouted once more before putting on Jevon's jacket while I headed towards the door. "Alethia, let's go I said", shouting even louder.

"Okay, okay, I'm coming", she said in her usual tone as she did whenever she felt she was being annoyed. "Excuse me?" I asked giving her my usual look that told her to take a step back and recognize that though I might be a young mother, nevertheless, I am the mother. As usual her apologetic stare told me she knew what time it was. She knew the deal as to what I was saying without even saying a word.

I was bewildered. My car was not there just the space where I had left it stared back at me. Looking around to see if I had parked it somewhere else, it baffled my mind. Where was my car? I remembered parking it, putting on the multi-lock just before setting the alarm. Where could it have disappeared? Grabbing a hold of Jevon, I ran back inside.

"I'm coming, I was just coming down", Alethia said stepping aside. From her body movements I could tell she thought I was coming to her because she took so long.

"My car is not there, I don't see my car", I replied ignoring what she said. Her expression change. Two seconds later my stepfather entered the building. He had taken my mother to work an hour before.

"Did you see my car outside this morning when you left?" I asked with hope.

"No, I wasn't even paying attention, where did you leave it?" his face showing concern.

"Across the street..." I pointed as though he could see through the wall.

"Are you sure?" he asked.

"Yes", I answered frustrated.

I did not know where to begin. I did not know who to call. I decided to first explain to Alethia that I thought someone stole the car and that I would be walking Jevon to school. I then told her my stepfather would take her to school when he took my brother, David, and my smallest sister Shanel to school. My mother had Shanel two years after I had Alethia. Shanel was spunky in every way. And aged beyond her years in attitude. I guess that's from being the youngest.

My thoughts drifted back to my car. Who should I call first?

After Doug and I decided that it would not work between us, I had started to speak more frequently to Steven again. I sometimes saw him during my lunch. We still had a lot to talk over. As I picked up the phone, I decided to call Steven instead of the police first. He would tell me who to call first and exactly what to do.

"Hi, Steven?" I said immediately as the person picked up the phone.

"Yes, what's up?" he was always there for me. Whenever I needed a shoulder to cry on, he would be there. Nothing ever dissuaded him from being a true friend to me. Even after he had moved to Texas, he had sent me tickets twice.

And after my job had kept moving me around to different locations, he bought me a cell phone and a beeper just to keep in touch with me.

Here I was embracing his friendship again, but this time I knew it would not be as before. Steven had really loved and cared for me but he had taken disadvantage of my kindness towards him. I could have been more understanding but I chose not to understand. He had a forgiving nature that I admired. He knew how to look beyond someone's fault and see their true character. As I fumbled for the right words to ask, I couldn't help but regret having gone back to Doug. A deep sense of hurt ran throughout my body causing the palms of my hands to ache.

"Well, what is it?" he asked again, but this time impatiently.

"They stole my car", I had tried being brave until now. The tears started forming within my eyes. I had tried to be brave because Alethia and Jevon was still at home. But now that I was alone I allowed the hurt to flow.

"Yeah right", he said as though he thought I was actually joking.

"I'm serious".

"From where?" he was appalled.

"Across the street, you know where the car dealer is? Right there". A year ago a car dealer had moved right across the street from where I lived.

"Didn't you put the lock on the gear stick?" he asked trying to understand how it had been possible.

"Sure".

"Are you sure?" he repeated.

"Of course", I replied.

"What about the alarm?" he asked.

"It was on. I remembered it was on because I took the computer to fix, when I returned home from the computer store I put the lock on, then I set the alarm", pausing for a moment, I then continued, "so I know I put it on".

"Did you call the police?"

"Not yet", I didn't know just where to begin. I was totally confused. Suddenly I did not know myself anymore. I could not see myself without a car. I didn't know how I would get to work. Going to Long Island from Queens was surely a long ride on the train. I did not know just where to begin. Work! I had forgotten. It was now 8:39 and I hadn't called my supervisor yet.

"Listen, I'm going to call my job, I'll call you right back".

"Okay".

My supervisor was not there but I spoke to another supervisor from another department. She was dumbfounded. The sympathy she gave brought me near tears. After I hung up the phone from speaking to the supervisor I called back Steven.

"Yeah", I could tell he had gone back to sleep.

"Steven?" I wanted to ask him to take me to the police station, but I did not know just how. My pride hindered me.

"What is it?" he was always straightforward in everything.

"Can you take me to the precinct?" the words finally came out.

"Sure", he always had a willing nature about him.

"Thanks Steven".

He was always there for me. I could always depend on him. Steven ceaselessly remained a friend to me regardless of anything and everything.

I spent the entire day making reports and contacting the insurance company. I never knew having a car stolen was so hectic. The representative for the claims division of my insurance company asked me questions that made me feel as though I stole my own car. The whole incident left me extremely stressed. After visiting the precinct I was told that they could not take the report there. That I had to call them from my house and the report had to be taken from the site of theft.

Steven took me back home and waited outside in his car. The ride to and from the precinct was quiet. He never spoke and I never said a word. My mind was filled with too many things that was going on in my life to be bothered with anything else. As soon as I reached inside the house I called the police. I somehow wished it a dream.

It seemed like forever before they came. I assisted in filling out two pages of the report, which helped to make the process faster. I invited Steven inside after they left. He had not slept much the night before. So now he lay sleeping in the living room. Alethia was already home from school. We both sat in the living room watching television as Steven slept. Steven slept quietly throughout the day. It was uncomfortable having him inside my house. Eventually he got up, washed his face and left. I was relieved. I enjoyed Steven's company but I did not enjoy his company so up close and personal any more.

I called Doug's job to let him know about the theft of my car but he was not available. The man who answered said he would give him the message as soon as he saw him. Throughout the remainder of the day I called all my friends to tell them what had happened. Everything about my life seemed to be getting worst. I felt as though I was losing control of everything. The thought brought about a fear in me.

The next day Doug called. After telling him what had happened he somehow did not seem appalled. He gave off no form of sympathy. Instead, he immediately accused Steven of having my car stolen. I was left in awe of his accusation. I couldn't help but wonder if Doug had gotten my car stolen. After speaking to Doug, I was convinced somewhere inside that he did get my car stolen.

Steven agreed to take me to work daily. He was always on time. Our friendship became stronger.

All morning I called Steven, but he did not answer his phone. Looking at my watch I realized that Steven was late. Pacing the floor in my living room I became anxious. Alethia had just gone upstairs to my mother's apartment. My stepfather took her to school in the mornings. Jevon had already gone to school. Now I waited anxiously for Steven to come to take me to work, but he was late. I knew he was on his way because he never broke his promises. Suddenly the doorbell rang, that had to be him. Grabbing my bag I quickly opened the door to meet him downstairs.

"Hi you're late", but after greeting him, I realized something was wrong. "What's the matter, are you okay?"

He looked pale.

"My stomach again", he answered holding onto the door.

"Come upstairs a minute, let me make you a cup of tea", I said turning back upstairs.

Once inside I called my job to let them know I would be coming in late. As I headed for the kitchen I could hear the growling sounds Steven made from the pain. He hugged the chair as the pain ripped him apart. He then knelt on the carpet with his head on the chair, crippled by the pain. I quickly made the tea and brought it to him. The front door of my apartment suddenly opened. It was my mother.

"Little girl, you didn't hear me knocking?" she asked in her usual authoritative voice. She always liked to think she had control, and I fed her womanly or should I say 'motherly' ego. I had not heard my mother's banging on the door.

"Steven is sick, his stomach hurts", glancing at him with sympathy.

"He need tea?" she asked.

Finally sitting down on the sofa, I turned around to face her, "No, I just gave him some".

"Oh", but before she could finish the doorbell rang.

"Who is that ringing my bell this early in the morning?" My mother hated people ringing the doorbell so early. She did not care whether they rang her bell or mine.

Heading towards the kitchen, she went to the intercom on the wall directly over the microwave.

"Yes?" she asked rudely.

"It's the police".

"We didn't call you, maybe you have the wrong address".

"Is this 109 Boulevard Place?" from the manner in which he spoke I knew he was reading it from a paper or book.

"Yes, but no one called you".

"Ma'am can you come down for a minute?"

"Sure", she answered him returning to us in the living room.

Steven had gotten up and was now sitting on the chair.

"Can you believe these people?" she said referring to the police.

My mother and I went down the stairs to speak to the police. Before I left I could see a sense of concern on Steven's face.

As she opened the door, the cops walked in, "We had a report that there was a disturbance on the second floor", he said looking down on the paper he held in his hand. There were three other officers standing behind him in the doorway.

"Sir, I think you have the wrong address", my mother insisted.

"No ma'am, this is the address we were given."

My stepfather soon came down the stairs and stood directly behind my mother.

"Well, its just me and my husband and my kids, she live on the second floor and I live on the third", she said referring to me. "But if you would like to come up and see for yourself....", she continued as she moved herself out of their way.

"Sure, thank you" the cop in the front replied as they all made their way upstairs behind her. The sound of their boots against the steps sounded like rushing horses. Looking around they observed the entire house. They must have been satisfied, because they all left. I wondered if Doug had called them and made a false report, but I decided to think otherwise. Suddenly that fearful feeling began to appear again.

"Listen hurry and put on your clothes so that I could leave", I could tell he too was suspicious. I hastily put on my clothes and we left. Steven was still experiencing extreme pain when we got in his car. He was sitting in the passenger seat when I finally reached down stairs.

"Still feel sick?', I asked just before driving off. But he did not respond, he instead made a growling sound from the pain.

As we entered the Grand Central Parkway he told me to look in the rear view mirror to see if I was being followed. I thought him paranoid. I knew then that he was thinking the same way I was. That Doug had something to do with the cops coming to the house this morning. Looking in the rear view mirror I saw nothing suspicious and sighed deeply. Waiting to enter the flow of the oncoming traffic, I moved cautiously into the middle lane.

Suddenly there was a hard bang on Steven's car. Shocked, I looked in the rear view mirror. It was Doug. He banged his car against ours three more times. Fear took hold of all the courage that I had inside. I suddenly felt weak. As I moved to the left lane, he remained to our right. I was relieved. I thought maybe he would have left us alone. But I was wrong. Speeding up to our car, he looked at Steven and me with hate in his eyes. He drove his car ahead of ours and moved quickly in front of us. Suddenly he stopped his car again beside ours. From the movements of his lips, he called me a B—. He then slammed his car in the right side of our car causing it to spin half way around twice—once to the left, then to the right. Steven held onto the steering wheel trying to keep full control of the vehicle.

"Watch out Kard, he's stopping for you to run into the back of his car!!!" Steven screamed.

Swerving out of his way, I stepped on the gas and tried to drive as fast as I could. But he still kept coming at us.

"Call the cops Steven, call the cops!!!" I screamed. Thank God Steven had a cell phone.

"Hello!, there is a man chasing this lady on the Grand Central", I could tell that fear had taken a hold of Steven as well.

"Tell them he's stalking me!!" I screamed.

"I think he's stalking her".

Doug still kept coming at us.

"Tell them he has a license plate number of xxx3301!!"

There was no reasoning behind all of this. Doug and I had tried one more time, but we both had come to the conclusion that it was not working. We had both outgrown each other. Things could never be the same for us ever again. The things that I had admired in Doug were not admirable anymore. And the way I use to be I was no longer that person—insecure, empty and searching for something to fulfill that emptiness. I had found the Lord. I had found something that gave me peace even when there was a downcast of storm surrounding me. Something that made me smile even though tears came rolling down. Something, that when there was yet no one around, I felt loved. Cared for. Wanted. Needed. Something, that set a bubbling kind of feeling way down deep. A certain something, that though I did not know what tomorrow holds, I was hopeful for tomorrow. Something, that took away all fears of evil. That something was God—the sweet beautiful aroma of God's presence. Of knowing that regardless of my faults, or if tomorrow I woke up without a husband or a friend, that some-one was there no matter what. So I was not the same. Couldn't be the same. And he found that hard to deal with. And I too found him hard to deal with, so we had come to a decision to be friends while we still had a good open communica-tion for Jevon's sake.

As I looked back at Doug's car coming closer I felt a fear of death within me. Steven was calm unlike me who nervously drove his car amidst the heavy traffic on this Monday morning. Doug had death in his eyes and revenge on the wheels of his car. I made my way to the Van Wyck Expressway, but Doug pursued us just the same. Heading towards the Belt Parkway he continued chasing us still. I was tired and fearful at the same time. I could not go on any more. I was weary from all the driving and the hitting of his car on ours.

Steven advised me to exit so he could drive instead. I would have preferred him driving because he was a much better driver. Exiting off the Belt Parkway was difficult because there were so many cars on the road, but eventually I did. As I made my way down 182nd Street and the North Conduit, I pulled over. Quickly I got out of the car but somehow procrastinated. Suddenly there was the sound of tires over the asphalt of the street. It was Doug's car. He had found us. He kept coming at full speed. Without hesitation, he slammed his car into Steven's. The entire left side of the back of Steven's car was disfigured. Without warning, Doug exited his car and made his way to where I was. As he approached me I stepped back but not before he slapped me in my face. Astonished I slapped back his face. He then made his way to the left side of the street, and picked up a white piece of pipe as he ran towards Steven's car. Steven must have saw Doug coming, because he left with the tires screeching against the asphalt. Doug decided to pursue the chase again.

I was left standing in the middle of the road confused. I had never seen Doug this evil before. I was worried for Steven. As I stood wondering where to go, I looked towards the highway for some sign of hope. Suddenly I heard the voice of a man calling.

"Need help? Want me to call the police?" It was an elderly man standing at his gate. He had seen everything. "Who was that?"

"My ex trying to kill me and my friend", I was in total shock as I tried to gather my composure.

I had read about it, heard about it. But never did I imagine the cry of being an abused spouse. He took me into his house where his wife had been waiting for him to return. She welcomed me in as she called the police. Her husband took the phone from her as he continued to explain to the police exactly what had happened. He was much taller than his wife. She was petite and beautiful. He weighed about two hundred pounds. They had pictures of their children all over their house. On their center table were two pictures of two children who had uniforms on. They apparently were in the armed service.

I asked the woman for permission to call my job to let them know what had happened. My supervisor answered, but I was unable to speak. Suddenly I was overwhelmed with fright and started crying. She could not understand anything I said. She told me it was okay and to gather my composure and then call her back.

The cops came within minutes of the call. They took the report but couldn't take an accident report because there was no evidence of an accident. Steven had left because Doug had chased him down again. So they did a report for harassment instead. I had called Steven on his cell phone. He gave me his location. The cops decided to take me to where he was so I could get my pocket book out of his car. I had not gotten a chance to get my pocket book before Doug had slammed into Steven's car. I thanked the couple and left with the cops to find Steven.

Upon arrival at the location where Steven told me he was, I saw an ambulance and a cop's car. I also saw Steven and Doug's cars. I was fearful to what might have happened. As I exited the police car I walked cautiously towards the other police car that was parked directly behind Doug's car.

The police officers that had taken me there also exited the car. They approached the cops on the scene. Their discussion seemed intense. They took forever or so it seemed. Walking towards them I could see the look of disbelief on the woman police's face.

"Come here this", she said beckoning her partner, "she is his wife".

I could read her lips and knew what she was saying even though she had whispered to her partner.

"That's not true", I called out desperately after her.

"Miss, you have to speak to them", she said brushing me off with her hands and quickly vanishing in her car. They drove off immediately. I had wanted to tell them the truth. The truth about Doug. That he had lied. Yes we were married, but I was not his wife. Only on a piece of paper. I had wanted them to believe me. But they had not. Slowly walking over to the other car that waited I bent my body low enough to see their faces.

"Excuse me, what did Doug tell you? Who's in the ambulance?" I was shaking all over.

This all seemed like a nightmare. But it was not. I had somehow wished that I would suddenly open my eyes and found out that this was just a bad dream. But the reality of it stared in my face as I looked on the two cars parked in front of me.

"Well, he said he's your husband, and he came and found you and this guy in bed".

My mouth fell open. Why was Doug doing this to me?

The police continued, "he claimed your boyfriend pulled out a gun at him and then when he picked up the phone to call the cops, you both ran downstairs and he chased you both. He said he was coming from a hard day's work".

I was in shock. Doug had lied and I could not believe it. I asked the officers if I could tell them what really happened. I was overjoyed to hear them say yes.

It all made sense now—the cops coming to our house earlier that morning. Steven telling me to watch if someone was following me. It all made perfect sense. Every bit of everything that happened that day Doug had planned it all. On the Grand Central he had blocked our car with his and had gotten out. He then jumped on the hood of our car and jumped up and down maybe three or four times. While jumping he had mentioned that he already reported us to the police so he could do whatever he wanted to us. He then used his foot to kick the windshield. When that didn't break, he jumped down and punched the window of the driver's side. That's when Steven had told me to drive off. As I drove away he once again punched the back window in his final attempt to break the window. His pursuit had started again.

It all made sense. I was not sure just what he had told the police wherever he had gone to file the false report. But I knew he had gone somewhere. After telling them my side of the story, they no longer believed Doug. The officer that sat in the driver's seat began telling me about his divorce proceedings.

A tow truck was called for both cars. They were unable to tow Doug's car because he had the emergency brake on. I asked the man who drove the tow truck to lend me his cell phone to call Doug.

"Hi, Doug, you okay?" I was frightened for him.

"Yeah, you?" he asked concerned.

"I'm okay. Listen, the man is about to tow your car but he cannot because you left the emergency brake on".

"Oh", he must have forgotten.

Then the man took the phone and began to explain that he could still tow it away but his tires would not be good after he towed it.

Doug showed up in less than ten minutes. I wanted to hug him, but I could not. I wanted him to tell me he would not abandon our friendship now, but he said nothing.

I knew going back to work would be the hardest. Facing everyone would be the most embarrassing thing I would ever have to deal with. Everyone knew. Hours after the incident I had called my supervisor and explained everything to her. She had gone around the office telling everyone out of shock and sympathy. She had advised me to make a report. I took her advice and went to the 115th station and made a report later that day. That's when I found out that Doug had filed a false report at the 110th precinct the morning before he trailed me on the Grand Central Parkway. He had told them that Steven and I had called the day before and threatened him with a gun. Detective D'Ante was put in charge of the case. He could not make an arrest because Doug had filed a report first. How could I let them see that he had lied?

The next day Detective D'Ante called me on my job to tell me that he was unable to arrest him because Doug had a different story to tell. I could no longer stay at work. I had to leave. My supervisor was at lunch, but I had to leave. I knew I jeopardized my job by not telling my supervisor that I was leaving but I just could not stay. Why hadn't they arrested him? I was almost killed. Couldn't they see the holes in his story? I knew eventually they would, because I would make them see them somehow.

I spent the next day at home trying to fathom a way to make them see that Doug's story didn't make sense. I suddenly remembered I had gotten Doug arrested before. I had called the cops on him twice before because of his violent temper. I decided to go to the precincts that had the reports and get copies then take them to Detective D'Ante.

I called my friend Anthony and asked him to take me to the precincts. I had met him at the Motor Vehicle office when I had gone to get my permit several years ago. We had kept in touch after that. I had invited him to church and he had visited on several occasions. Doug had threatened him too. He had threatened to 'punch his face in'. Anthony had just laughed at him. He never really took Doug seriously.

As we drove to the different precincts trying to strengthen my case against Doug, I explained everything to Anthony. He always understood. Maybe because we were only friends. He listened keenly without interrupting and gave sound advice. He was engaged to his children's mother and had been for over six years.

We went to three different precincts, including the one where he had placed a false report. I gathered the evidence needed and returned to the 115th precinct. Detective D'Ante was impressed and saw my determination to prove Doug a liar. He decided to call him in for questioning.

Doug was called into the 115th station. He was questioned. Three days later Detective D'Ante called me on my job to let me know he decided to arrest Doug. He decided to arrest him on his job. I was overjoyed. That's all I had wanted. This way I would be listened to in court. Doug needed psychological help and he needed it desperately.

But things got worst after Doug came from jail. He called my best friend, Tiffany and threatened to go to my pastor and her husband if I did not withdrew the charges.

Eventually he did go to my pastor, because I was persistent that I would not withdraw any of the charges. When that failed he went to his son's mother and lied that I had used her social security number and her name to get jobs. And what was worst is that she believed. As much as Doug had lied to her and cheated on her, she believed everything he said. He told her I was illegal in America, the only truth he told.

However, what he did not know was while he spent time in jail I had went to the Immigration and Naturalization Service office and gotten approved for my green card. He did not know that I was no longer illegal. I had brought all the papers from his past arrests and the present and they had approved my case immediately.

Days passed without me hearing anything more about Doug. A deep feeling of fear clutched my inside as I wondered what other plans of evil he was up to. I prepared myself for anything.

My mother must have heard the door slammed behind me because she quickly came downstairs.

Just then the bell rang. I was startled because I just came and there was no one behind me.

"Who is it?" my mom asked through the intercom.

"Detective Johnson", the voice shouted.

Why would a detective be at the door? I thought as my heart fluttered.

"Who?" she repeated.

"Detective Johnson, is there a Kard living here?" he asked.

"Yes, one minute". My mother got up from the table in the dining room and joined me in the kitchen.

Fear controlled my thoughts as I made my way down the flight of stairs wondering if Doug was behind this once again.

"Yes?" I raised my brows as I cautiously opened the door.

The man at the door was about five feet five inches. He had very little hair on his head and a receding hairline.

"Detective Johnson", he said flashing his badge open.

"Come on in", I said as I glanced downwards to notice the yellow envelope in his hand.

"What is the problem?" my mother interceded.

I was glad for her interruption and her show of support.

"No problem, I am here to give Ms. Kard this supoena", he said unfolding the letter in the envelope and then handing it to me.

Quickly running my eyes across the paper I then showed it to my mother. It was a supoena from the Assistant District Attorney's office. Doug was due in court in two days. I had thought they had forgotten all about our case because it was almost two months since I last heard from the lady at the Assistant District Attorney's office. She had offered me a cell phone in case of an emergency, but I had refused the offer. After all it could only dial 911.

The supoena stated that I had an appointment to state the facts of the case two days before he was schedule to appear before Assistant District Attorney. Immediately bitterness began seeping into my heart so I knew I had to pray before I went.

After the Detective left, my mother cautioned me of Doug and told me to do what was right for Jevon and me. She then shared out a serving of ackee and codfish with dumplings, my favorite meal, the national dish of Jamaica.

As I entered the big glass building on Queens Boulevard a demon of fear approached me. But I quickly cast it aside and focused on the Bally's Fitness Club that stood welcoming me through its doors. Ladies with towels loosely wrapped around their necks wandered in and out. I thought, someday when I could afford the luxury I would become a member.

As I made my way to the receptionist on the ground level of the building I opened the letter to see the name of the Assistant District Attorney that I was coming to see. I introduced myself and asked for Mrs. Chambers and went to sit and wait. It seemed like forever until a petite-framed lady stepped towards me minutes later. The receptionist was right it did take a couple of minutes. I had doubted her because in the business world, a couple of minutes could turn out to be hours.

"Hi, I'm Mrs. Chambers and you're…?" she trailed off glancing at the paper. But I quickly interjected and completed her sentence.

"Kard Robinson".

"Yes this way please", she said beckoning me to her office.

As I entered her office I sighed heavily. I just wanted to get it over with. I no longer cared whether he stayed in or out of jail. I just wanted to get it over with and move on with my life.

Her office was immaculate apart from the numerous boxes that lined the wall along the window filled with sheets of yellow and white papers. On her desk were two pictures of two children, the little girl resembled her and had the same dark colored hair as she did, but the boy had a blond colored hair with blue eyes. Maybe they were her kids. Just then I noticed the wedding band on her left hand and a picture on the wall behind her. It was a much larger picture than the ones on her desk. The man in the picture looked exactly like the boy on her desk. That must be her husband and the children her kids.

She asked me several questions about Doug's past and about our marriage. She concluded eventually that what Doug needed was counseling, not jail time because he would come out worst than he went in. She said if he was given jail time he would loose his job, which would make him bitter and become a further menace to society. I totally agreed.

As I exited her office, I glanced at the clock on the wall above the receptionist's head. The meeting only took forty-seven minutes, but it seemed like two hours. As I exited the building on Queens Boulevard a sudden gush of wind brushed against my face. My life began strolling through my mind and I realized that other than my two children, I did not have anything of importance in my life. I wanted more. I wanted more for me, and more for them. I longed to be able to afford vacations every year and not worry about paying an electric bill for $30.00. I knew one day though I would make it happen just for them.

The train took forever to come. I was glad that there were only two other passengers aboard. As I entered the train my mind wandered to Steven. We had become very best friends since the past month. Steven had matured and began communicating more with me. He had been in a relationship that went sour which caused him to see me in a totally different light. He used to think I was miserable because of inquiries of his whereabouts, but now he knew that I had only cared when I questioned him so much.

Just then my phone rang.

"Hello", I said as low as my voice could go, glancing around. I hated answering the phone in public.

"Wha'pen?" he replied with his usual happy tone.

"Nothing, I'm on my way home. Everything went okay", I was always happy to hear his voice and to see his face. I knew I shouldn't be with him because I was a Christian, and he wasn't. But I loved Steven and could not stop loving him.

"I have something for you okay," he said sparking my curiosity.

"What?" I asked inquisitively.

"I'm not going to tell you," he teased.

"Okay, I'm coming right now okay". I could not wait to see what he had. He gave gifts from his heart and they were always expensive.

The train seemed to take forever to reach. I rushed up the steps and made my way towards his house. The door was already opened. I slowly walked up the stairs to catch my breath. Then I tapped gently on his door.

He grabbed me around my waist and pulled me to him. His kiss was wet and firm. He was the one for me but I was afraid. I was afraid to love him because he was never settled. He hardly stayed home. He was always hanging out with his friends and I already had problems with trust. Holding my hand in his, he placed a small box into the palm of my hand.

Pulling away from him I opened it slowly. It was a diamond engagement ring with a wedding band to match.

"Will you marry me?," he asked smiling. "I want you Kard", he continued.

I could not believe a player like Steven was now ready to get married. I wanted to say yes but I feared that he would still be the player that he was. But how could I say no when he has been there so long for Jevon, Alethia, and me. He waited patiently to hear my answer. Should I? Could I?

The Promise Land

They desperately tried to cross the borders of Africa to Morocco, trying to reach the Promise Land of Europe. Cardboard boxes became their beds and the woods of Africa became their commode.

Some are caught and deported if they even make it to Morocco alive. Others must spend their counted days wondering how to face the Promise Land. But they must pay their way. And money was not to their avail. So they must seek diligently while living off the rots of Morocco's streets.

A six by seven room becomes seven men's house and one bed is shared by them. So they must take turn sleeping in each day that is made into several shifts.

The journey to Europe from Morocco is a trying one. Only the brave and the lucky survive. Sometimes even the brave will die. The sea claims him and his companions aboard their sometimes-unstable boat. They must pray for strong tides to welcome them and not be fierce towards them. They must seek pardon from the master of the sea. And if granted then they must flee the men of the sea. For if captured, they are brought back to Morocco's shore and deported to Africa for sure.

But some are determined. And they will fight Africa's desolate desert, and Morocco's bitter shore. They will press to fight the raging tides to make it to the Promise Land. Their once full face will eventually show their protruding cheekbones. And their once moist lips will soon be cracked and brittle by the salt air from the sea. Their once slender bodies will somehow become meager. But they know they must go on.

Sometimes many months will pass and they will only know the lining of the shores of Morocco yet still. And they will wait for their perfect second, perfect minute, perfect hour to pledge to the master of the sea with their lives. And finally their hour may come. And if it does, they will face the many challenges that they must somehow defeat and conquer.

They will somehow make it to the Promise Land. And if they do, and when they do, they are sometimes greeted by pebbles of sand and rushing tides. And a smile will adorn their faces and they will look to the sun and thank the master of the sea.

The master will run away with the tide to greet another African. On the soil of Morocco they'll stand. But then the sun will ask, "Now what?"

Earth Angel

I have two children, a daughter and a son. My daughter is the oldest. My son is only six months old. In my attempt to salvage what was left of my marriage I got pregnant. Months before my conception, I asked my Pastor for advise. He advised me to stay in what I knew to be a doomed marriage. My marriage no longer existed emotionally. My husband had stopped providing for us financially. Things was tough because I was not working. Each day my day started with me taking my daughter to school and ended with me contemplating my future.

This day was no different. As I took her to school as usual she walked ahead of me instead of beside me as she normally did. She had gotten upset after not being able to take lunch to school. I told her to eat at school, though I knew she was allergic to one of the ingredients they used to prepare the lunch. I was forced to tell her to eat it anyway. I told her to eat the fruit and drink the milk. I had no money to buy her lunch. I had no money at all. I was broke.

Watching her enter the building of the school, my heart wept. She turned around to look at me in hope that maybe I would tell her that I would bring her lunch, but then she held her head down as she saw the obvious—she really had to eat the school's lunch. She continued to hold her head down as she walked away and vanished amidst the rest of children entering the building. My heart ached terribly.

As I pushed the stroller with my son, I knew tomorrow could not repeat today. I knew I had to get some bread and maybe a ninety-nine cents package of salami or ham from our neighborhood supermarket. I stopped to search my purse. Like I had suspected I found only two dollars. This was the two-dollar bill that I had gotten from a customer as a tip when I worked at the Jamaican restaurant prior to my conception. I hastily made my way to the supermarket.

"God, you know if I was not serving you I would just take whatever I needed for my daughter. But I cannot and I will not fail you. Because you said whatever I need you will supply. I am standing on your words. You said heaven and earth shall pass away, but your words are forever. Provide for me please. And if not for me, for the innocent child."

As I tread through the halls of the supermarket I noticed that they had bread on sale and the ham, two for eighty-nine cents. I suddenly got an urge to pick up juice, milk, cookies—stacking the basket that I carried and that I had straddled over the handle of the stroller. As I made my way, in faith, to the check out counter, I felt somewhat embarrassed, but God comforted me within.

I was next on line.

After the cashier scanned all my products, she looked at me with a smile and told me my bill was fifteen dollars and eighty-seven cents. I gave her the two-dollar bill I had. She waited with her palms outstretched.

"Ma'am, I need thirteen dollars and eighty-seven cents more."

"I'm sorry, that's all I have," I replied softly.

"Excuse me?" she asked, her smile turned into a frown.

"That's all I have," I repeated more confident this time.

"Do you need a supervisor?" she asked.

"No. Not really," I answered because I knew all the supervisor I needed was in the God I served.

"Excuse me", she said out loud to customers behind me. "I'm sorry", she continued, "Can you please move to another line? I have a problem here."

"I don't have a problem", I whispered.

Everyone became frustrated. I never bothered to look around but I could hear disgust in their voices as they scrambled for the next cashier.

"What's the problem?" his voice was deep and calm. I thought he was the manager.

"That's okay Sir", the cashier replied as she picked up the phone next to her register.

"No Ma'am, really, what is the problem?" the stranger insisted.

"She can't pay her bill", the cashier explained to him as she pounded the buttons on the phone.

I started praying silently. My son still slept.

"How much is it?" his voice was soothing when he spoke.

The cashier rolled her eyes towards the ceiling and replied, "she owes thirteen dollars and eighty-seven cents more."

I could no longer take the embarrassment. I thought God would have interceded already. Maybe the sale at the supermarket was the blessing God intended.

"Give her back the money she gave you, and take this," handing her a twenty-dollar bill.

That's the only time I turned around to face the stranger. He was standing a foot away yet his voice sounded as though he was in a much closer proximity. He was a Caucasian man in his late sixties or early seventies. His skin was very wrinkled. He had blue eyes that glistened. His eyes deceived his years.

He held two cans of cat food in his hand. The cashier returned my two dollars and I squeezed it into my pocket. I thanked him a million times. Someone had left two cartons of orange juice on the side of the register. Handing them to the cashier, he told her to add them to my bill.

"Orange juice is good to prevent the common cold" then he walked away after putting the thirteen cents change in the container that held the tips. He didn't bother buying the food for his cat.

Hurriedly, I grabbed my bags and rushed out the store to thank him again. As I exited the store, just seconds after he left, he was nowhere to be seen. Two ladies stood on the sidewalk discussing current affairs in Guyana. I questioned whether they had seen a Caucasian man existing the store. They insisted no one left the store. As I walked away securing the bags to the handle of the stroller, I heard one say in a Caribbean accent, "She crazy, what a white man doing in this neighborhood, an' a ole white man at dat? She 'ave to be crazy."

Inspirational...

Why me?

Why must I bear all these temptations?
Why me?
Why must I bear so many trials?
Why me?
Why must I hear the gossip?
They say—she'll never make it
    She'll never make it
        She'll loose her way.

the WIND is blowing again

I must be determined
I must pass the test
There is so much hope in God
So in him my faith should rest
> but there are times when I get tempted and tried
> and I failed the Lord one more time
I don't want to be blown away
with every wind that blows
I don't want to be cast down with every storm
> I don't want to be blown away
> with every wind that blows
I want to stand on solid rock
I want to stand on solid rock
I must stand on solid rock
On solid ground!
> I must be determined!…

joy again...

I have found my joy again
Look...
I've been blessed again
I've been set free

I have found my joy again
This time around...
it's for Eternity

I have found my joy again
This time...
I wont reject his love and grace
I have found my joy again
I'm on my way to see him face to face

I have found my joy again
now I'm on my way to see him face to face

unconditional

why HE still love me?
i don't really know
why HE still cares?

why HIS grace still shine on me?
why HE has restored my faith?

'cause i had brought HIM shame
brought HIM so much pain
yet HE still love me

unconditional love HE gave
when HE took me back

again

my Salvation

I can remember
the day of my salvation
when the cares of this world meant nothing more to me
when the joy of my salvation
was my reason to live
Then my mountains turned to valleys
And I was cast in

But I will rise
Out of my valley
Then all my joy
shall be restored
Yes I will rise

I will rise
Out of my trials
I will rise to eternity

I will rise

There was a time
when joyful singing
turned my darkest clouds into sunshine
there was peace within
Now my joy it's all shattered
And my peace torn apart
But I will rise
To see the Glory of my Lord

Then I will rise

I will rise out of my trials
I will rise

Because I know that he loves me
I will rise

?

What can you do
when life's problems get you down?

Who can you talk to
when there's no one around?

When burdens get too heavy
and they're too much to bear

who do you call
does anyone really care?

Pressing On

I know sometimes
Life gets so hard
It seems as if you've been fighting
just too long
I know sometimes
Things gets so rough
And it seems as if you just
Can't go on

But you've got to walk
Or you've got to run
But you must do whatever it takes
To win this race!

Blessed

I must confess
That I'm truly blessed
Because of you
Because of your love
I am blessed
I must confess

Overcoming

I shall overcome
All of life's problems
All its mishaps
All its fears that cause me to run

Still I know I must trust in God
Because he alone is my refuge

So today
Though I am down
I shall overcome
I shall overcome

HE REIGNS FOREVER

When I think of where I could be
I give praises to God
When I see
The less fortunate than me
I give praises
When I wake up to behold the sun
And the clouds are gone
And the rain has ended
And a new morn has begun
I see a rainbow with its colors
Promising me tomorrow
And then I remember
Where I could have been
And Calvary stood
With stains of blood
And I know it's me
That should have died
But he took my stead
And I waiver to serve him
And he waited for me to come
And I came
Then went
And I returned
But felt—
—Nothing
Now nothing can hold me back
Because I have found my place
As his child, a prodigal
You see
He lives within

Me
A new creature
He is my Savior
One day we will be together
Because he saved me again
After the former, again
After the latter, again
And I will rise to serve him
Because he lives within
Me
A new being
Because he is my King
He reigns forever
And ever and ever
When I think of where I could be
I praise God
And shall throughout eternity

Moving On Up

I was wretched and torn
Shattered and bruised by sin and shame
Blight by iniquity
Yet he called my name again
He gave his life for me
To save my soul
And that is how I knew
From that day on
He was my God

Now I'm back on my way
I am moving up and up
To behold success
Nothing shall stop me now
No enemies, no obstacles
Step back
Step out
Step aside
Here I come
I am coming to take what's mine
I am conquering on
And on

Mount Calvary

There is no one in this world
That can take the place of him
There is nothing in this world
That can give peace like he gives
When I first met him
He whispered in my ear
I died for you
On Calvary
Have no fear

My feet were shackled
My hands were bound in sin
I had stray away
One more time again
But he waited patiently
He said, "I knew you would need me"

Through the hurt
Through the pain
He welcomed me back again

Won't Give Up

No one knows the loneliness
That surrounded me
At nights I'd cry to God up above

In the day I was strong
But when the sun was gone
The child in me
Came alive
But God kept me warm

Why would I want to give up now?

The road behind me
Still seems so long
But looking ahead
It gets shorter home

Why would I want to give up now?

When I remember
Trials and temptations
It had to be God
That pulled me through

Why would I want to give up now?

I've been through too many valleys
To give up now
I've won many battles
Because God made me strong

Why would I want to give up now?

When the tides were high
And my ship was caught in the storm
The lighthouse led me on somehow
Why would I want to give up now?

Why would I want to give up now?

Waiting Patiently

When my Pastor said another one
Would be walking down the aisle
My heart sank to the floor
Another chance for me just went by

Was I not good enough?
For God to bless with the other half of me?

Then God whispered and said,
"Keep worshipping,
Your blessings are closer than it seem."

When the job of my dreams
Didn't come through for me

God said don't worry
When the house of my desire
Didn't come to reality
When my food supply went short
And a dollar was all I know

He whispered and said:
"Keep worshipping
Your blessings are closer than you know.

I am not a God of hast
I am God who is sure
Forever.
So don't worry my child
Worry No More."

Trials

Trials will come
But we must praise his name
Forever just the same

He said he would never leave
Nor forsake

So in the valley
I will call on him

Wounded and bruised
My faith was torn apart
My dreams were no more
But his words kept me strong
They were for sure

Believe in his will and his way
Then you will know
He'll fight your battles
And if you are still
He'll destroy your foes.

Because of him
My today's battles are tomorrow's victories
My today's valleys
Are tomorrow's mountains for me

Memories…

Dandy Shandy

We would save the empty boxes
The pint milk boxes that is
Then we would stuff it with newspaper
And made sure the edges were gone
By knocking the edges in
But if they intended to play a real game
The edges then remain

And when it was my turn to face the war
I would tuck the hem of my skirt in the legs of my panties
Making it a shorts
And I would make sure my legs were strong
Because before I started I'd bend all the way down
And then I would know the strength of my legs
By standing straight
Because how strong I was determined my fate

And if I could just make it to five
And if I could just make it to seven
And if I could just make it to nine
And if I could just make it to ten
I'd win

But the ball always hit me
Because they knew my style
So as I stood in the mirror before the game
Different styles I tried

Then there was the call
The game had started
It was my turn to face the challenge

in honor of the great Bob Marley

The greatest singer on earth
was Bob Marley
For he sang the best
I'd leave school on the very hot days
And visit his studio

The gates stood high
With lions guarding each post
And as you entered you heard his songs.
'Lively up yourself'
played loud
and I longed to hear
'No woman no cry'.

For when the pain of the heart
Settles within your soul
Bob Marley's song
Would give you hope.

No woman don't cry
Better days are coming
No woman don't cry
Today's just passing

No woman don't cry
Hold your head up high
Though life shows
No more reason for living
No woman
No woman
No woman

Don't cry
No more

Off to Sunday School

Their big broad hats to match their shoes
And their pocket books,
Their elegant attire
Coordinated color,
They're off to Sunday School

And the road to the church is steep
Upon a hill
And the asphalt unknown to them
And the rocks
Beneath their spike heels
Feels their weight on them

And the church doors are open to greet the guest
To see the return of the Saints
And the ladies with their big broad hats
Step proudly up the stairs

And when they whisper to each other
Because now they're in a Holy Place
And their gestures to each other
Is filled with Grace

And they must hurry
To find their familiar seat
Before a visitor sits there
And they must worry
If the children
Will destroy their frilly socks with a tear

Christmas in Jamaica

When i was nine
I loved Christmas time
For I got to see the parade
and the john-ku-nu-nuhs
And the men on the tall sticks
that held them high

And the funny mask
That hid the faces of our fellow countrymen

And the mask that had the faces of our heroes that died
Sam Sharp, Paul Bogle, and Marcus Garvey
came first
Then one by one the other heroes
came dancing out

And the way they jumped from side to side
The mask seemed very heavy
As it controlled their heads
And I was afraid of the funny-faced men

But now that I'm grown
Christmas comes too soon

And what is everyone happy about?

Back Home

People always mistake one for the other
Their rough skin protects the delicate flesh inside
Medium sized black oval seeds decorate the soft inner layer
Hard scalloped patterns design the outside of both fruits
Black spots randomly hide amidst the deep green outer surface
Their similarity deceives many people

The two tropical fruits differ in sizes
The sour sop weighs more than the sweet sop

The sour sop or Sapodillas as other Caribbean natives call it
Makes an excellent beverage
In Jamaica it is used to prepare a Sunday drink
Though edible without any form of preparation
It harbors a bland taste
The usual weight varies from two to five pounds

The sweet sop gained preference amongst children
Because of its sweet but subtle taste
Easier to maneuver while eating because
The seeds are easy to remove if the fruit is ripe
The flesh of the fruit then melts itself away from its pit
In your mouth
And with each bite
Trickles of juice flows from your lips onto your hand
And then the children take their tongues and lick the juice
From the sides of their hands
All the way down their arms.

I couldn't believe

The party was nice
My sister said that
I thought it was okay
The men and women danced the night away
They danced really close to each other
My sister and I laughed together
To see the vulgarity of the men and women
Dancing so close together

It was nasty
That's what I said
She said they were having fun
The lady in the blue jeans was pressed against the wall
As the man prevented her from moving

The spot where she stood
Had blue dye on the wall
He must have pressed her hard
Poor lady
That's what I thought
But my sister said it was just a dance

I could never dance like that
My sister and I agreed for once
We could never dance like that
No matter what
Such vulgarity
To be pressed against a wall-
Insanity!

the TINY Soldier

The living room was an island for him

and the pictures on the tv
stimulated his imagination

he fought many wars
and conquered many lands

his tiny fingers held their guns for them

and his mouth carried their sounds

miniature feet ran above the ground

and he hid behind barracks that looked like chairs

he knew they could not see him

he knew they could not kill him

he knew he would win the battle
because he was lord of his game.

The Seaside

I was too small for them to play with
So I played by myself
I squeezed the sand between my toes
And watched as the boats came in
Sometimes the water greeted me too
Then kissed my feet goodbye
I gazed beneath its blueness
Till it leave the sand again dry

The men would scramble with their nets
And their prized possessions caught
And with glee in their eyes at the women who came
Money sounded in their throats when they laughed

And the women came
To observe their goods
Some nose upturned with scorn
Some barefooted, head tied
Some swearing its fresher at dawn
And the boats came in one by one
And the men couldn't wait till it reached the shore
They waddled in the water
And pulled on the ropes
To beat the others
To greet the groups
To sell their stocks
Caught in the deep
While I lay in bed fast asleep
That's when the water always begin getting rough
And I know its time to go home

And I would tell the water goodbye
Until tomorrow again

THE OLD MANGO TREE

SHE SAT BENEATH THE OLD MANGO TREE
TOO OLD TO BEAR ANY FRUIT
HER FACE STAINED WITH TEARS
AS SHE PLAYED WITH HER BARE FEET

EMBROIDERED WITH THE DIRT
THAT HARDENED BE'TWIX HER TOES

FROLICKING THE ROCKS AMIDST THE DIRT
SHE THROWS THEM WHEREVER THEY FREELY GOES

HER DRESS TOO SHORT, TOO TIGHT
LAY DAINTILY ABOVE HER KNEES

THE VILLAGERS PASS HER TO AND FRO
NO ONE SEES HER DREAMS

SHE MUST HEAR THE "YOU AIN'T WORTH A PENNY"

AS THE SUN LEAVES HER ONCE BLUE SKIES

SHE MUST SEE THE HANDS RAISED HIGH
TO SLAP HER TENDER FACE

SHE MUST SEE DESIRED LOVE
REPLACED WITH WORDS OF HATE

AND YET SHE SITS BENEATH THE SHADE
OF THE OLD MANGO TREE

AND TASTE THE SALTINESS
OF HER RIVER ON HER FACE THAT RUNS SO FREE

Sweet, Sweet Tobago

I long to go home
To the glass bottom boat
Where two miles into the sea
The water is four feet deep
I long to go back home
Where the tourist roam
Amongst the dead coral reefs

I long to go home
To the small island Tobago
Where not many things are said of
Where the sun is warm
and the breeze is cool
And the people wear a smile all day long

I long to hear
the natives speak
And drink the coconut water
And ask the man
To crack the shell
And eat the white flesh inside

I long to taste the tree-ripe mango
And bite into the ripe yellow skin
I long to visit sweet Tobago
I longing
I longing
Oh boy I longing!

Dear Mama
(Jamaican Dialect — Patois)

Dear Mama,

How yu doing?
I am fine, su how is fahrin'?
Can yu sen' mi a new pair a shoes?
School start in Septembah
An' a new bag fi gu pon mi back
Please Mama remembah

Daddy sey fi tell yu
Him really miss yu
Miss Marlene she fi ask yu
If yu find di vacuum

Mama when yu coming back
Is ten years now
Mi t'ink yu sey yu just a gu
Fi mek some money fi help wi out

Mama mi nu t'ink yu a come back
Many night mi cry
Nuff night mi siddung an' wondah
Why Mama left mi, Why?

Write me back soon
Mi a du good in school

Mi love yu Mama,
Always yu daughtah

Dear Mama
(English Version)

Dear Mama,
How are you doing?
I am fine
How is America?
Can you send me a new pair of shoes
School begins in September
And a new back pack
Mama, don't forget
Please remember.

Daddy says to tell you
He really misses you
Miss Marlene says to ask you
If you remembered her vacuum?

Mama, when are you coming back?
It is ten years now since you left
I thought you said you only went
To make some money to help us out

Mama, I don't think you're coming back
Many nights I just cry
Many nights I sit and wonder
Why you left. Mama why?

Write back soon
I'm doing good in school

I love you Mama
Love always, your daughter.

Missing You

I miss my grandpa more than ever
Now that Christmas is here
Now that the apple pie
has filled each room
And everyone sings good tidings and cheer

I so miss my grandpa
More than ever
Now that the leaves are gone
And the trees are bare
And the wind feels cold
And I hear grandpa's favorite song

I miss my grandpa
More than ever
He brought love at Christmas time
I so miss my grandpa
More than ever
He brought the warmth like rays of sunshine

MAMA

Her wrinkled face
always carried a frown
Though nothing kept her down
Her ash gray hair
Her daring stares
Her name was MAMA

The way she walked
and dragged her feet
You knew how far, how near.
The pinnacle of our family
Everyone sought to be like her
And her name was MAMA

And we called her MAMA
because she was our heritage
—MAMA
She held our past
And carried our present

MAMA

5 LINCOLN TERRACE

CHARLIE YU MADDA CALL YU
T'REE TIMES OR FOUR
CHARLIE YU MADDA WARN YU
DON'T MEK SHE CALL YU NO MORE
COME WASH THE DISHES SHE SAY
AND WIPE UP THE SARDINES
THAT YU SPILL ON THE FLOOR FROM YU DINNER DISH
COME MEK HER HOUSE CLEAN

CHARLIE YU MADDA CALL YU
LOUDER THAN BEFORE
CHARLIE YU MADDA SAY
IF SHE CALL ONCE MORE
THE BROOM STICK GONNA FEEL YU BACK
AND THE SHOES HEEL
SAY HELLO TO YU HEAD
CHARLIE I SEE HER COMING
RUN CHARLIE!
OH GOD!

CHARLIE YU BETTER GO NOW
STOP PLAYING HIDE AND SEEK
MS. MARY SAY TO TELL YOU
SHE WILL TAKE CARE OF YU NEEDS
STOP WALKING SLOW
HURRY UP
AND LOOK LIKE YU IS SAD
MY GOD I JUST CAN'T BELIEVE IT
HOW YOU SO FOOL YOUNG LAD

LISTEN WHEN YU REACH
SAY
MAMA HIM NEVER TELL ME
THAT YU DID CALL ME

SHE HAVE A BROOM AND
A RED HEEL BOOT
WAITING FOR YU SKIN
CHARLIE I DID WARN YU, YOU KNOW
BUT AS USUAL YU JUST DON'T LISTEN

OUR AFRICAN VILLAGE

THE RAIN PATTERS AGAINST OUR ROOF
MADE OF THIN SHEETS OF ZINC
AND IT FALLS ON THE DIRT
BETWEEN OUR HOUSES

AND IT FALL ON THE FEET
OF THE CHILDREN IN OUR STREET
THAT PLAYED IN THE DIRT
BETWEEN OUR HOUSES

AND IT FALL ON THEIR HAIR
THEIR UNCOMBED HAIR
AS THEY DANCED IN THE STREET
MADE OF DIRT BETWEEN OUR HOUSES

AND IT PLAYED A RHYTHM
WITH THEIR VOICES
AND IT STRUMMED A MUSIC WITH THEIR WORDS
AS THEY PLAYED ON THE STREET
MADE OF DIRT
BETWEEN OUR HOUSES
AND THEY'RE FROM AFRICA
THEY SPOKE BOMBARA.

My Grandfather's Cry

He came home from work at nine o'clock
Every day
His presence was known by the loud banging of the
Iron gate
As he slammed them together
We knew he was in the house when the second
Iron gate that led to our veranda slammed
And then the door, the front door would proceed.
My grandmother always said,
"Hell, this ain't no prison door
why must he slam them so?"
but he never heard.
She kept her silence and listened to the
Refrigerator door slammed as he took
His dinner out to warm it on the stove
For in those days the word microwave was never known.
And he would warm his dinner in the yellow container
With the little green border on the rim
And she would say
"Must he slam everything so
my God the food maybe hit the floor"
but she never said a word loud
for it to be heard.
And the TV would start talking
and his silence could be heard in the living
room
And when he finished eating
He would come into my room
And he would cover me gently
With my sheet on my bed

And my granddaddy would say
"Mitchy?"
cause that's the name he would call me
and he would say as his tired eyes stared into my innocent eyes
"You know your daddy love you right?"

Dear Granddaddy,

I miss you so
If I had known
When I was young
That I wouldn't have you forever
I would have stayed with you forever
I would have gone to work with you
I would have done your work for you
I would have made your dinner for you
And my grandmammy wouldn't wash for you
Because I would have done all that for you
And I would have cut your hair
And not the barber man who told you stories weird
And I would have told you I love your beard
When you didn't want to shave.
And I never would have said
"Granddaddy why is so face so rough?"
I would have rubbed my delicate face
Against its roughness out of love
And I would have gotten your slippers for you
When Popeye and Olive cartoon was on
And I would have gone to get the water for you
Though you said 'Mitchy that is okay'
And I would have cried with you
When grandmammy had to give you pills
Because your belly hurt so much
And I would have laughed with you
When I didn't understand your jokes
And I would have tasted the drink you made
Though as you tasted it
You wrenched your muscles in your face

And I would have held your hand as I walked down the road
Not just the street to cross
And I would have written you notes
And left them in your room
So you could see them after work
And I would have played with you more
And I would have talked with you more
And I would have called you my granddaddy more
But now you're gone.
Sometimes I feel you near me
And I want to touch you.
And I hear you call me.
And If I had known
That soon you would have gone
I would have told you I love you
before you could tell me you love me
And let you know granddaddy that you will always be my granddaddy.

Missing you

If you're hearing me
Know that I love you

If you're seeing me cry
Know that I care

If you're standing afar off

And your presence surround me

Know that I miss you so much

I know you're in heaven
And I know you watch over me

But I miss you here on earth

I never really got to say goodbye

To be FREE…

FREEDOM RINGS

Just to be free
once more—

Just to be able to fly
once more—

Just to be free
once more—

Just to have wings
once more—

Tomorrow

God gave me gifts
to explore this universe
To enable the self
To transform minute things
To vast capabilities
But if I utilize not the gifts
Then my existence existed not
And I'll leave the world empty
And nothing in history marked.

If tomorrow I awoke
And unable to utilize my brain
Then today I would think
Of things beyond my thoughts.

If tomorrow my eyes were blinded
and nature's beauty hidden
Then today I would see the bird fly
and a rose petal opened
I would see the GLORY in the sky
or the ant upon their hill
I would see the wings of a mosquito
Fluttering a million times.

And if tomorrow I could not hear
the wonders of this world
Then today I must hear
The wings of a bee buzzing
And I must hear the rushing
of the sea shore

And I must hear the wind against the leaves
and I must hear nature's silence.

If tomorrow I knew
my gifts would be taken away
Then today I would establish GOD's gift
in unusual exciting enticing ways.

I Will Rise

Each morning I must rise
to face the challenges of this life

Some write 'within her there's no love'
Others speak 'she'll never find love'

They question my love
Seeking explanation for my love
But I will rise above their questions
Their assumptions
Their inquisitions

I must be strong to go on
I must be me despite the odds
against me
I must seek to devour every negativity

I must conquer the land around me
Because I am free
Just to be me

Therefore

I will rise

First Step

I had been married before
Hurt before
Cheated
Deceived before.
I swore never again
Not this life
No one's wife.

Then he walked in
unannounced.
From Africa sent by the wind

He left his desert, gold, nation
He came to find me
To steal me from hurt
To protect me from deceit.

Now as I learn to trust the winds of Africa
As I set my eyes on the motherland's gift
It's Black Opal
It's Gem.
I feared fear itself
I search for a reason
Why
Why
Did I allow all my wouldn't's
Into DO's

But my heart is saying go
My fear is saying stop
My feet moved away from the other.

My first step towards trust.

Just One

Two different countries
Two different cultures
One soul

Two different religions
Two different nations
Yet one soul

Two worlds apart
Two different languages
But one soul

Mary Beth/Sue

Every workplace has one—
a Mary Beth or Sue
who makes life completely difficult
carrying to the boss bad news
and I often wonder
how good this place would be
if Mary Beth or Sue
suffered a casualty
and couldn't come to work
because of a broken leg
or lost their voice permanently
and had to 'sign' instead
Then everyone would see
the snitch they are

but then I was brought back to reality
by their voice afar

Open Cage

To write is to release
To capture a moment
before it gets away

To ruminate and tell the whole world
To feel and let others feel
To know and let others know
To feel what others feel
but scared to say

To know what others think
But dare not say
because inhibition within them
won't let them write to say.

Oh let me write my soul away
let me release
release me
the caged me.

Me
Being released.
Release my soul.
Like the birds amongst the clouds
Release me.

STRANGER IN THE PARK

The stranger stopped just to say
hi
My son came running with questions in his
eyes
He stood tall as he faced
The Stranger
and then replied:

> We have a pet
> We have a pet frog
> A little one
> But he died.
> [with sadness in his eyes]
> Do you have a pet?
> He asked The Stranger

Yes The Stranger replied
I have a wife
a pet wife
That's a big pet my son exclaimed

Then The Stranger said
Bye.

The
Drunk

He staggered across the road like a drunken man
But I was too far to see for sure
     He held onto the plastic bag he carried in his hand
And it seems as if the wind would carry him away
   But he held the ground with his feet
     The asphalt knew he would stay

And the bag in his hand seems to hold his dinner
    But I was too far to see for sure
      And he cherished the grip with a smile now and then
And I thought the bag would fall
    But he held the food with his thoughts
    And the contents thereof

And he finally made it across the street
    And he thanked his faithful feet.

The Green Card Theory

Be careful
And don't get caught up
With a Brother Man

    Who doesn't have a green card
    Or work permit in hand

Be careful
And don't give your love
To the Brother Man

    Unless he has a black book
    Stating he is a citizen

Only love a Brother Man
When his life is already complete
Only give your heart to him
When sure of his motives

I know because I trusted one
From West Africa's Land
A deep mahogany Brother Man
Trying to get one in his hand

THE iNNER MAN

MY HEART CRIES
MY SOUL WAILS
MY SPIRIT SAYS SOOTHE ME.

MY PEACE SHIVERS
MY JOY SHAKES
YET MY SPIRIT SAYS STAY.

MY HAPPINESS BLACKENS
MY GLADNESS UNRAVELS
BUT MY SPIRIT STILL SAYS

KEEP THE FAITH BLACK WOMAN
LET THE MOTHERLAND'S GREENERY
WITHIN YOUR SOUL SHINE ON
SHINE MOTHERLAND'S DAUGHTER.

SHINE ON.

the Question

I asked hm what he thought
occupied my mind.

        His mind wandered but for a second.
     Then, with gleam in his eyes
        He said love.
No I replied.
        Why he questioned?

Think again you must.
But all he could think of was love.

      That's it.
        That's all my mind knows to say.
        Love.

LOVER'S QUERY

I LOVE HIM?   I LOVE HIM NOT?

'TIS THE QUESTION ASKED.

MY HEART SCRAMBLES FOR AN ANSWER

MY SOUL WRESTLES WITH ITS THOUGHTS.

OH DECEIVE ME NOT.   GIVE ME AN ANSWER.

TO COMFORT THE WOMAN IN ME.

I MUST KNOW THE TRUTH AT ONCE.

I AM FACED WITH INTENSE CALAMITIES.

MUST I GO?   WILL I STAY?

IF I HAD TO LIVE AGAIN

THIS CHOICE WOULDN'T BE.

FOR IF IT WOULD   NOT TOO QUICK

BUT NOT FOR ETERNITY.

THE DREAM

I HAD A DREAM I HID FROM THE ENEMY

I SEARCHED FOR PROTECTION

TO FIND PEACE BUT NONE CAME TO ME.

THEY SOUGHT ME TO DEVOUR ME

I RAN AND HID HOPING THEY WOULD NOT FIND ME

MY HEART POUNDED HEAVILY

AGAINST THE PURE WHITE LINEN ON THE BED

MY ENEMIES LOOKED DESPERATELY

IF THEY FOUND ME THEY'D WISH ME DEAD

FEAR CONTROLLED EVERY MINUTE OF MY SLEEP

A KNOT FORMED IN MY THROAT

ANXIETY INCREASED.

THEN I AWOKE.

I'M MY LOVER'S ARMS.

LOOKING AROUND—NO ENEMIES, NO HARM.

WHAT DID IT MEAN?

THOUGH ONLY A DREAM!

MY THOUGHTS REMAINED UNSETTLED!

VANISH ENEMIES—VANISH!

What is LOVE?

WHAT IS LOVE?
HE ASKED. BUT I JUST LISTENED THEN.
I HAVE HEARD OF IT, READ IT, WROTE THE WORD EVEN
BUT NEVER UNDERSTOOD.

HIS EYES WANDERED ABOUT
EACH CORNER OF THE ROOM
HE HELD HIS CLASS
SEARCHING FOR AN ANSWER
TO HIS QUESTION

CAN ANYONE SAY—
-—HAVE YOU BEEN IN LOVE?
EXPRESS YOURSELF,
TELL EVERYONE!

ANYONE?

IT'S A PECULIAR THING
A SPLENDID THING
YOU MUST TRY IT
YOU MIGHT LIKE IT.
LOVE.

WHAT A WORD.
NO ONE RESPONDED.
NOT ONE SOUL ANSWERED.

OKAY,
LET'S MOVE ON.

HE GAVE UP.
LIKE EVERYONE IN LOVE.

JUST GIVE UP.

THINKING OF YOU

I SPOKE ABOUT YOU TODAY
TO MANY ON MY WAY
I SPOKE TO THE BEAUTIFUL INDIAN PRINCESS
WHO LISTENED
I TOLD OF YOUR CHARISMA
AND THE WONDERFUL MAN YOU ARE
I MENTIONED YOUR CHARACTER
YOU'RE ONE OUT OF A MILLION STARS.

I SPOKE TO THE WISE PROFESSOR
WHO TAUGHT ME
THE MEANING OF THE WORD LOVE
I TOLD HIM OF YOUR WISDOM
A GIFT FROM GOD ABOVE
I WHISPERED TO HIM HOW I LOVE YOU
ESPECIALLY THE WAY YOU SMILE
I TOLD HIM HOW YOU LOVE ME
AND DO SO WITH GREAT PRIDE

I SPOKE TO A CHILD
WITH NOT TOO MUCH YEARS
NOT TOO MANY CARES
BUT OH HOW SHE LISTENED.
AND I TOLD HER OF MY NEW FOUND LOVE
HER YOUTHFUL EYES GLISTENED
THEN SHE SAID WHERE IS HE
NOT TOO FAR AWAY I SAY
SHE PAUSED TO THINK WHERE TO BEGIN
BUT GAVE A SMILE INSTEAD

I SPOKE TO A HEART—
—MINE WITHIN
BUT IT KNEW EVERYTHING
IT TOLD ME OF MY LOVE FOR YOU
AND WHISPERED SOMETHING MORE
IT SAID THE LOVE YOU GIVE ME
IS A PEACEFUL WAVE
REACHING UPON MY HEART'S SHORE

SILENT WORDS

IF TIME COULD ROLL BACK FOR ONE SECOND
THEN MY WORDS WOULD NOT HAVE BEEN HEARD

THEY WOULDN'T HAVE PIERCE YOUR SOUL
THEY WOULD HAVE REMAINED IN MY THOUGHT

THEY WOULD HAVE BEEN LEFT ALONE
BUT THE SECOND ROLLED TO FORM

A MINUTE

AND MY THOUGHTS BECAME WORDS
AND MY WORDS BECAME AN ARROW

AND THE WORDS DREW BACK THE ARROW
AND THE ARROW FLEW FROM THE BOW.

THE STRANGER in MY BED

As he lay sleeping
As the dead on their back
I looked within him
Trying to understand.
He was a stranger
Yet I know him.
I tried to see if I could live without him
But a deep feeling of loneliness
Surrounded every organ within.
I did not know him much
Yet I was his wife.
I had taken a vow
To be with him for life.
As he snored deep in his sleep
I wondered how foolish I was.
To not know this stranger
Yet give him so much love
At times I wish it wasn't
But then how can I run
Our lives had already begun
To take its course
To set the pace
What would our fate be
I long to know
I wish to see
In our future
Just what it would be????

Fah-Rin

ME A GO A FAHRIN
ON A BIG BIG PLANE
ME A GO A MERKA
AND A WON'T BE THE SAME
MY COLOR WILL BE LIGHTER
AND I'LL LEARN HOW TO TWANG
MY MADDA BOUGHT ME NEW CLOTHES
FOR THE TRIP TO FAHRIN
CAN'T WAIT TO SEE THE SNOW
THEY SAY ITS LIKE CRUSHED ICE
I'LL MISS ALL MY FRIENDS
BUT I WILL SEND YOU SOMETHING NICE
NOTHING IS EXPENSIVE YOU KNOW
AND ALL THE STREETS ARE GOLD
NO GARBAGE IS ON THEIR STREETS
NO HOUSES OVER THERE OLD
EVERYBODY IS RICH RICH RICH
AND THEIR SCHOOLS ARE VERY BIG
NO UNIFORMS JUST CLOTHES
EVERYDAY THEIR WEAR
MY MOMMY SAY
HER HOUSE IS BIG
IT EVEN HAS AN ELEVATOR
LAWD! I CAN'T WAIT TO SEE
THE BIG CAR MY DAD BOUGHT HER
I'LL SEND YOU PICTURES
AND A LITTLE SNOW
BUT WAIT—
—WON'T IT MELT?

JUST KEEP THE JUICE AS A SOUVENIR
GOODNIGHT—ME GONE TO MY BED.

Jamaica Airways

THE plane landed around 7:30 p.m. I was startled by all the hands clapping throughout the plane. The lady who sat beside me explained that they clapped in celebration of their safe arrival to the USA. The trip from Jamaica seemed like forever.

THE sight of Queens above the ground made my adrenaline pump faster. There were lights everywhere. The plane seemed to circle for three hours before the wheels finally hit against the asphalt. Though it only took five minutes.

EVERYONE appeared to be moving slow though they hustled to vacate the plane. The small bag that I carried still remained in the overhead compartment.

FINALLY I exited and made my way through customs.

I was fascinated by the tone of the Custom Officer's voice. I couldn't wait to learn to speak like him. He wished me good luck. When I answered my tone differed extremely. Especially when I tried to imitate him.

THE door swung open and my uncle stood behind the iron bars that separated the travelers from their friends and families. His eyes glistened as he recognized me. I guess mine did too. I guess mine began glistening after I boarded the plane in Jamaica. And I know they never lost their gleam.

OUTSIDE the cars moved fast and the horns honked loudly. We dashed across the street and made our way towards the parking lot where his car was.

WE both kept silent. As he drove out of the lot my eyes wandered everywhere. There were lights everywhere. Bright lights. And the streets were huge. And the streets were the size of three streets put together in Jamaica.

THEN I smiled because I knew I was finally here in America.

Survival

I gotta take demeaning jobs
To pay my bills and feed my kids

I have to lay beside a man
Ain't got no feelings for
To pay my bills and feed my kids

Gotta listen to Auntie Mae
For the twenty dollars today
To pay my bills and to feed my kids

But one day I will stand and walk away
From the demeaning jobs
The man I ain't got no feelings for
And Auntie Mae
Telling me my history
Just to get a twenty
To pay my bills
And
Feed my kids.

Diff'rent?

If I was a diff'rent color
Would life deal me these cards?
If my hair was a little straighter
Would I have gotten the promotion?

If I ate caviar
Drove a Rolls Royce car
A chauffeur
Would I be noticed then?
Would I be happy then?

If not—
Don't wanna be
Born

Again.

Selling out

He's a black man
With that black man's walk
Trying to play the other man's game
Trying to fit in
Trying to win
At any cost
Any other man's lost
As long as he makes a name

He's the ghetto kid
With the ghetto kid's grin
Trying to speak
The other man's language
He lies with words for
His voice to be heard
He deceives his own
For gain alone
As long as he assumes the win

But must he let us wear the
Shackles
Again?

The chains on our ankles again?

But must he teach us to say
'Massa'
Again?

Must he?

Must he?

As long as he wins?

Loveproof

As I lay beside you
With your arms around my chest

The body that bore your child
Resting against your breast

The rhythm of our heart beat
As you caressed my soul with your silence

> I didn't need to ask you if you loved me
> I felt it in your presence

As your tongue showered my body
No longer youthfully refined, defined

Its sculptured definitions absent
Because it bore your child

Your manly passion filled me
Your strength erupted within me

> I didn't need to ask you if you love me
> I knew I was your queen

Ain't my mama's fool

Not because I love you
My mama ain't raise no fool

Not because I cater to you
My mama ain't raise no fool

Not because I give you pleasure
At your beck and call

Not because I wine and dine you
My mama ain't raise no fool at all

Not because I scream your name
And tell you I'd die if you should leave

Not because on your birthday
I maxed my credit card bill

Not because the sneakers you wear
Cost me half my pay check

Not because your boys came over
And I stayed cooking in the kitchen

Not because I found you creeping
With the neighborhood's 'hoe next door

Not because I stayed with your sorry a—
My mama ain't raise no fool for sure

Not because I gave you the keys
To enter my apartment

When you know for sure
You ain't paying rent

Not because I gave you my car
And not a dollar for gas you spent

Not because I never mentioned
That you gave me nothing on Valentine's Day

Not because our anniversary passed
And I chose silence
'cause I ain't got nothing to say

Not because for three days
You stayed with your auntie
I knew nothing about

Not because your shirt
was stained with lipstick
But it came from your friend's girl's mouth

Not because you think I've been a fool
For the years we've been together

My mama ain't raise this fool
To be a fool forever

Bye!

The Vow

My lover and I quarreled
our honeymoon ended
three days later
where is the love?
I shouldn't have said I love you.
I do.

What is forever?
What is for better or worse?
Was this the worse?
Or is there more worse?
In sickness and in health.
Sickness?
What sickness?
Mental?
Physical?
Mental!
I shouldn't have said I do.
I should have waited.
We should have been friends.
What is a friend?
For better or worse.
Friend.
In sickness, in health.
Friend.
I shouldn't have said I do.

To my daughter, With Love

Take all the time to be a child
Don't worry
Your womanhood will come
For once the child in you is gone
You can't turn back the clock

Braid your doll's hair
make clothes for them
Out of scraps
Mix mud for soup
And use play dough as bread
Cherish your childish heart

And boys, they could wait
They're here forever
Believe me—I wish I knew
I'd adore my youthful days till now
I'd treasure them just a little more

Trespassers

His uniform was full black
with red patches on the sleeve
his coat was shiny black
with a splash of white color on its beak

He guarded his territory
high above the ground
from a post that carried a light
he frequently gave his signal sound

If you listen carefully
you would know that he was there
but for those who were too busy
or didn't listen—
because they did not care

As they trespassed through his path
he would leap towards their head
to let them know that they were standing
on his bought and paid for land

Runners hopped in fright
bicyclists terrified, rode from his flight
but none could escape.

Tune of your Heart

Play the tune of your heart,
Sing loud its melody,
Why must we be afraid?
Take a step.
Be free.
Express yourself.
Be open.
Let your soul reign and shine.
Rise to greet the rays of youth,
within you lingering on.
On.
And on.
And on and on.
Express yourself!
Be not afraid.
Shout it loud.
Be brave.
Be brave.
Play the tune of your heart.
Play the tune of your soul.
Shout it out loud.
Watch everyone follow.
You and you and you
And you.

Who decides?

Another woman conceives—
Another abortion?
Another child?
Another child is born.

Another doctor?
Another teacher?
Another drug dealer?
Another drug addict?
Another caught up in our system?

Another who?
Another what?
Another brother?
Another?
Another?

Wind Cold

I hear the wind
and feel the breeze
it whistles as it dances through the trees

It reaches near
and brush my face
it rushes though in a race—to touch my skin

Its coldness passes through my soul
as I wondered from whence it came
No scent it carried
Just bitter cold

Go away wind
Go back home

Without a Name

she struggled each day
to make a way

no one knew her name

to the world she did not exist
to life she stood still

no one knew her name

she fought hard to become someone
everyone would recognize

yet no one knew her name

she wondered if one day
she'd be given fame

but today no one knew her name

Until...

We lay on an old blanket
I found in the trunk
the green leaves above us
reminded us of the prosperity of love
we said nothing
    But we knew everything

The wind kissed our cheeks
as it pranced about us
His head lay on my thighs
looking upward to the sky
His eyes were perfect brown
as his glance turned towards my eyes
    But we still said nothing

My hand explored his face
and brushed against the hair on his face
the roughness of them enticed my palms
I knew he was my man
The beauty of him danced inside my heart
    And we still said nothing

The peace of our surroundings
elevated our love
The silence of the air
captivated our soul
    Yet we said nothing.

the river guides me

Though the ground beneath my feet
scorches through my sole

Yet the river guides me

Though the sun above my head
sends its rays to pierce my soul

Yet the river guides me

Though the moon in its darkest hour
sends its light to blind my path

Yet the river guides me

Though the stars amongst the skies
sends its gleam towards me in parts

Still the river guides me

Though the universe spins around me

The river still is guiding me

Though other galaxies unknown exist

I know the river will guide me

SunSet

This morning
I rose to greet the sun.
To greet the moon
before it left the horizon.
To greet the Prince of West Africa's Land
as he lay asleep beside me.

This morning
I rose to kiss the morning dew
that fell upon the grass.
To kiss a new opportunity
that lay within my grasp.
To kiss the Prince of Mali.

This morning
I rose to feel God's gentle breeze
that dance upon the window sill.
To feel the delicate petals
of a rose still within its bloom.
To feel the warmth of Africa's gem.

Then the sun greet the moon
and the moon greet the sky
above West Africa's Land.

The Wedding

As the music hummed
And I walked to him
My father on my arm

In the pew stood my friends
And I knew we'd soon be one.

Perched

The bird on the windowsill
Another came to meet him
She flapped her wings
to show her happiness
Of being with her love again

They must have somehow got separated
Because he came first
Then she came second
And at first he seemed lonely
But she provided him company
And now they sat together
On my windowsill

I wonder what they thought
Or what he said to her
I wonder what she envisioned
Or did she speak great words

I need to know how birds do sing
such beautiful melody
And how they fly the skies in groups
In such awesome unity

Because my lover and I
We are one
And that's how it will always be
As we join the birds that stood still
On my windowsill

Shine Like The Sun

I see the sun
and the sun sees me

It warms the coldness within me
Each ray pierces my soul
Like an arrow shooting from a bow
They shoot happiness, peace, and joy
They shoot love within my soul
And then I become someone new

And I shine
Yes I shine

MEADOW PARK

HE SAT IN A CHAIR
BENEATH THE SHADE OF A TREE
THE BREEZE
BRUSHING AGAINST HIS FACE
AFTER WRESTLING WITH THE LEAVES
IN TUNE WITH MOTHER NATURE
HE ALLOWS HIS PALMS TO GREET THE SUN

THE GRASS TICKLES HIS SOLE
AS HIS SHOES BECAME STRANGERS TO THEM
FROM WHERE HE SAT
HE SEEMED QUITE STILL
ONLY THE SOUND OF THE LEAVES
WALTZING WITH THE WIND

HE KEPT HIS EYES CLOSED
AS HE FOUND INNER PEACE
THEN SLOWLY HE CHANTS
AS HIS MOUTH OPENS—SOMETHING
HE SAT THERE YET STILL
FOR ANOTHER SHORT WHILE

HE TOOK A DEEP BREATH

HE FOUNDED PEACE WITH HIS INNER CHILD

THEN HE EXHALED…

pondering

Today is only as bright
as you see the sun

The world is only friendly
Where your friendliness begins

A question remains a question
When no one chooses to answer

Miracles remain doubtful
Without fervent prayer

CIrcumcIse

I could hear her scream
from the pain
caused on her

She never asked to be born
In Africa's land

Why must she suffer so?
Why must her pleasure go?

And then they held her down,
All four of them

While the fifth performed his task
and he snipped so quickly
with his scissors
I hadn't heard the metal

But I did hear her scream
And I did see her blood shed
And I knew she would no longer feel
The pleasures of a woman

Fly away Freedom
Fly

Behind the glass I watched freedom fly
swerving amidst the sky

its awesome gravity

tranquility

Fly Freedom

Fly away
from this captivity

Fly Freedom
Fly far away

Freedom
D N
A C
E

Play the drum
Mr. African
Rise up to redemption
Sing the song of Africa's land
Strum the notes of freedom

Dance the dance
Our ancestor's dance
When their shackles were broken
Write the stories
for our children
So our history's not forgotten

Let your body send a signal
As you walk with head held high
Let your shoulders
Cry out a message
To the ones who say
"NEVER Brother"

We've come a far way
our Freedom is now
So forever Brother
Rise up and dance
The Freedom dance now

By the river

She struggled up the hill
And then down the rough rugged path
With the clothes bundled on her head
As the asphalt on her feet scorched
She must make it to the river
Before the other women do
She hated their gossips
Of men sleeping with women
Spoken in parables

Her frail body
Her weak eyes
Yet her strength was of a lion
For she knew she had to reach the river
To wash clothes for her children

She dropped the clothes on the ground
Tested the water with her hand
Satisfied
with the temperature
She stepped in the river
Grabbed the clothes
Pounded them with rocks
Without much soap

One by one
She washed
One by one
She rinsed
All at once she stopped
and held her back

She sighed
A loud sigh
Her load was still heavy
But she knew she had to finish
She knew she had to wash
the very last piece
in the bottom of the pan
For she knew they were the only clothes
Her children had

Celebrity's Letter

Dear Fan,
I wish I could prevent you from buying their paper
From listening to the gossips that they randomly scatter
The way they have dissected my character
The way they have scrutinized
Anathematized
Putting me with Tom, Harry, Moe, Larry
and Dick
The way they watch me
Concocting how to capture me
On paper
They have slandered me
Saying my partner's guilty of infidelity
Surely he doesn't want me
That's what they say
IN their paper
That's their pay day
What a way
To make a living
Sinful!
I wish I could sit and chat with you
To tell you the real deal
How it feels
To me
Wish I could walk around
Talk about
my business
Would be in the paper
in a second, minute, or hour
My business sells

For the right price if you tell
What I tell you now
I wish I could somehow
tell you about the columnist
How it really is
They take a simple hello
And say that I'm a Ho—
—Hold that thought
I just wish I could tell you somehow
but could I trust you though?

Celebrity's Mind

I just sit here
Bet my fans think that maybe I'm at
Some glamorous party
Bet they must think I never get sad
Or feel lonely
Or feel the blues
Or lack someone saying "I Love You"
But I'm just like you
Sometimes money ain't enough
It just causes hurt
It brings forth vipers
So called friends that connives
To get a dollar in their pockets

Sure wish I could release the real me

I cry sometimes in my sleep
My pillow taste my tears sometimes
My moans are louder than my cries
Like a child
I yearn to be a friend
To forget my fame
To forget my name

But can't forget my face
Because as I step out
Trying to be normal
They come
surrounding
taking pictures

Don't mean to be mean
But what you see
Is not always what it seems
The way you make your living
Is the same way I make mine
When you go home at evenings
Your work stays behind
So when I've finished performing
That's the beginning of my evening

I just want to get away
Be forgotten
So I can have a life close to normal
Please understand
I do love you
You're my fan

But I just want to live a life
As close to normal
As I can.

A Child's Cry

Who can I tell?
Mommy please,
Can you please just listen to me?

He touched me
Where he shouldn't have
He told me not to tell anyone

He said I was a bad little girl
That no one cared about,
He said you wouldn't believe me
You would kick me out.

I am hurting Mommy
I don't know whom to tell,
Mommy please
Just listen to me
He touched me again and again.

My heart is beating faster
Each time he visits us
And when you went in the shower
Again he started to touch
Can you please not let him come
To our house again
Mommy please,
Listen to me
He is a very bad man

Nursing Home

Every day is just the same
I have no place to go
I remember days gone by
I did things on my own

Now I must sit and wait
Till my food they bring
No one cares enough
To come by to visit

Days gone by
I had a job
Career and well-financed
Now I must sit alone and wait
For assistance

They feed me well
My clothes are clean
My sheets are changed
But I have no family

I was just too busy
To have a child or two
I didn't find the time to date
When I was proposed to

Now here I sit
Alone and old
In a nursing home
Waiting just like every day
For my Nurse Aide to come.

Growing Years

Relish in your youth
Explore the possibilities that awaits you
Embrace the challenges that are before you
Let each day ends with a lesson learnt
Learn to try instead of saying 'can't'
Welcome the coming years to maturity
Exert time to adore life's beauty
Smell a flower
Count the stars
Reaching for them though from afar
Develop self-confidence
To believe you can do anything possible
While you're young
Youth is a bridge from the unknown
Leading to ambitions of what can become
Reality of a dream
Or something that may have seem
Impossible
But you can achieve
Anything
So when the years have come
Welcome them
Know that you have overcome challenges
Because to grow old is not to wither away
But rather
To become more knowledgeable with each day
It is not possible to have youth
And years of knowledge
Or knowledge without years of challenge

I went to live with my granddaddy and his wife when I was only eight months old. He called me 'Mitchy'. Every night before I slept he told me he loved me. My grandfather was a strict disciplinarian. He only wanted the best. This book is dedicated to my granddaddy. He taught me self-respect and how to love myself. He retired and moved to Heaven, March 2000. What a man he was—strong, courageous, dedicated, and committed.

In loving memory of my grandfather (Daddy),
Nathaniel Adolphus McLeod
Who instilled within me dignity, morals and principles.

June 17th, 1927–March 2000
I miss you Daddy

978-0-595-39220-9
0-595-39220-2

Printed in the United States
51380LVS00005BA/250-276